Whispe

The Lost Legacy of Benjamin Chaires

By Sharyn Heiland Shields

Manufactured in the United States of America

Typeface: New Times Roman

Printing and Binding: Rose Printing Company

Library of Congress Control Number: 2015956763

ISBN: 978-1-889574-27-1 (Paperback)

ISBN: 978-1-889574-29-5 (Hardback)

Sentry Press
424 East Call Street
Tallahassee, Florida 32301

TABLE OF CONTENTS

Acknowledgments   v

Introduction   ix

Epigraph   xi

Prologue   xiii

Chapter 1
Maryland, North Carolina and Georgia   1

Chapter 2
East Florida   13

Chapter 3
On to Leon County   31

Chapter 4
The Benjamin Chaires Resumé   37

Chapter 5
Benjamin Chaires and Slavery   77

Chapter 6
Death, Family and Beyond   87

Chapter 7
Verdura   95

Chapter 8
The Youngest Son   123

Epilogue   137

Appendix   139

Bibliography/References   199

Index   231

ACKNOWLEDGMENTS

My deepest gratitude to the staff at Sentry Press:

Robert Holladay for his support, encouragement and facilitation of the publication of this book.

Dr. William Rogers for his wonderful sense of humor and for his insight and support.

Karen Wells for her valuable assistance with the layout and graphics for this book.

Marjorie Holladay and Jesslyn Krouskroup for editorial assistance.

Raymond and Sandee Vickers

And to...

Barbara Mattick for being a true friend whose interest in this book brought it to the attention of Sentry Press.

Mentors Glen Doran and Rochelle Marrinan of the Florida State University Department of Anthropology who gave me the confidence to enter the Master's Program in Archaeology and who encouraged me all along the way.

The St. Joe Company for allowing access to the Verdura site for preliminary archaeological projects.

Kay Porch, Abraham Prado, and Jennifer Wood of the St. Joe Company for their kind assistance.

Shane Fuller and Bill Weir, formerly with the St. Joe Company, for their support of, assistance with and interest in projects completed at Verdura.

Anne Marsh for scanning assistance.

Joe Knetsch for assistance with Spanish Land Grants.

Amber Pepe for her expert help with the bibliography and index.

Miriam Spalding and Claude Kenneson of the Florida State Archives.

Robert Ellis and George Shaner of the National Archives and Records Administration, Washington DC.

Gordon Thomas of the Ina Dillard Russell Library at Georgia College, Milledgeville.

Charles A. Tingley of the St. Augustine Historical Society.

Staff of the Washington Memorial Library in Macon, Georgia.

Staff at the Baldwin County Clerk's Office in Milledgeville, Georgia.

Staff at the Laurens County Library in Dublin, Georgia.

Staff at the Wakulla County Clerk of Court's Office in Crawfordville, Florida.

Appreciation is expressed to Chaires descendants who shared their memories, collections and friendship: Hank and Ellie Chaires, James B. Johnson, Joseph Dickerson, Don Shears, Anne Mintz, Elizabeth Barron and Janice Brown.

Special thanks to Chaires descendant Daniel Fletcher without whom this book would never have been written.

For projects at Verdura:

> Volunteers and Members of Panhandle Archaeological Society at Tallahassee (PAST) who participated in a clean-up of the Chaires family graveyard at Verdura on January 20, 2007: Ginny Hardcastle, Rhonda Kimbrough, Lonnie Mann, Laura Kammerer, Dave Ferro, Scott Edwards, Thadra Stanton, Tom Baird, Bill Stanton, Claude Kenneson, Ed Green and descendants of Benjamin Chaires, Janice Brown, Victoria Brown, and Jessie C. Shuford.

> Volunteers and Members of PAST who participated in an excavation of the North Structure February 19-21, 2010: Tom McClusky, John Roberts, Jerry Davis, Tom Baird, Fred Gaske, Mary Pat King, Andrea Repp, Lonnie Mann, Ed Green, Dennis Sittig, Steve Martin, Dorothy Sousa, John Grant, Rhonda Kimbrough, Alec Potter, Thadra Stanton, Richard Allen, Caroline Claiborne, Laura Kammerer, Dave Ferro and descendants of Benjamin Chaires, Janice Brown and Jessie C. Shuford.

And…

All my love and thanks to my husband Thom Shields for his never ending support, encouragement, good humor, and patience.

INTRODUCTION

My first experience at the Verdura site (8Le1211) was in 1965 or 66 when I was an undergraduate at Florida State University. Some friends and I were on a Sunday drive when we came upon a dirt road leading into the woods. We parked and started walking down the road. Soon, we were surrounded by planted pine trees, not very exciting, but we continued on our walk. All of a sudden, one of my friends said, "Wow! Look at that!" I turned to look but didn't see anything but pine trees. Then, as I kept looking, like a 3-D optical illusion emerging from an otherwise indecipherable set of dots, two sets of brick columns appeared. We ran to look. We found a huge pile of bricks between the columns. Where were we? Who lived here? Then, suddenly, we saw the graveyard (8Le4192) and ran down the hill toward it. Enclosed by a brick wall, there were several grave markers, some stately and impressive, others smaller and less opulent. Who were these people? Why were they buried out in the middle of nowhere? The only clues were the names on the markers, but the people in the graves were unknown to us.

Fast forward 10 years. I had graduated, earned a Master's degree in dance and gone on to travel around the country, studying dance, performing, camping out and learning to be an adult. After a not-unusual-for-a-young-person bad life decision, I came back to Tallahassee to sort myself out and begin to seek professional employment. During that time, a newspaper article appeared in the Tallahassee *Democrat* on January 25, 1982 which described the Chaires mansion house and included a photograph of the columns. Bingo! It was Verdura Plantation, the mysterious place we had explored all those years before.

Fast forward another 10 years. I was still in Tallahassee, still dancing but getting a bit restless—wanting to do something else, but what? I had always been fascinated by archaeology but really knew nothing about it. Why not take an introductory class? That class led to two field schools, upper level undergraduate and graduate course work and eventually a Master's degree in

Anthropology with an emphasis in Historical Archaeology. In one seminar, we were asked to present a paper to the class about an archaeological site. I asked our professor if anyone had done any work at Verdura. No. OK—that would be my chosen site. On the day I gave the presentation, there were about five entries on my timeline for the site, but that was to change. My thesis, an outgrowth of that seminar project, was completed in 2001 and was entitled *The Verdura Place: A Historical Overview and Preliminary Archaeological Survey*. As I began working on this book, the timeline that had started with only five entries soon grew to over 10 pages and seemed to have a life of its own, getting longer every day. I now have multiple file drawers, several flash drives, and dozens of computer files and notebooks full of Chaires research data.

It has been the most extraordinary experience of my life to have had the opportunity to research Benjamin Chaires, his family and his plantation and to discover and record the stories from their past. It is my hope that this book will provide a heretofore missing part of Florida's published history.

Verdura...

- ❖ *The sliver of a breeze whispers the past in your ear*
- ❖ *A shadow reaches for your shoulder*
- ❖ *Your foot treads gently on small things swallowed by the earth*
- ❖ *Faded memories of other days*

PROLOGUE

Scene: a dimly lit bedroom in a stately but still unfinished mansion. The room is stuffy and hot with windows closed; the stench of sickness and sweat are overpowering. Family members are crowded around a four poster bed where a middle aged man is suffering from the end stages of Yellow Fever: bleeding from the eyes and nose, jaundice, unbearable fever, extreme diarrhea, coffee ground vomit, delirium, confusion. He's been sick for over a week but felt better a day or so ago. Today he is much worse. House slaves come and go bringing poultices or implements for burning sulfur. Bloodletting by his doctor hasn't helped. Nothing helps. Death is inevitable, and he finally succumbs to it. Slaves set about preparing his grave, to be the first in the Chaires family cemetery, not far from his deathbed, at his plantation, Verdura. The inscription on his monument will later read:

> Sacred to the memory of
> Benjamin Chaires
> who died Oct 4, 1838
> Aged 52 years 8 mos and 9 days
>
> His many virtues are deeply
> engraved on the hearts of
> those friends from whom
> death has prematurely
> torn him, and by whom he
> can never be forgotten.
> His purest epitaph their tears.
>
> Blessed be his spirit.

His obituary appeared in the *Floridian and Journal* on October 6, in the Apalachicola *Gazette* on October 20 and in the

Florida *Herald* of St. Augustine on October 25. He was described as being

> endowed with an intellect of a highly superior order—a close observer of men and things—with a strong fund of practical good sense, aided by experience, and being reflecting and prudent, a high value was placed upon his judgment by all who knew him. By a course of industry, economy, prudence, punctuality, and strict probity he acquired in early life extensive credit, by which he was enabled to amass a princely estate. . . . He was a kind and affectionate husband—a fond and indulgent father, a warm friend, an [*sic*] useful citizen, and a good man. . . .

Chaires had been one of many migrants from Virginia, the Carolinas, and Georgia, who were drawn to Middle Florida during the 1820s. The rolling hills, the abundant water in creeks, rivers and lakes, and the inexpensive fertile lands were enticing to farmers and planters who had worn out the soil in their native areas and were looking to increase their wealth in the warmer climates of Florida. Ultimately, Chaires became part of a group of elite, wealthy planters with many ties to the new territorial government. But Chaires stood out. His ambition took him in many directions socially, economically and politically. He was engaged in business activities beyond the plantation, and he was highly respected for his civic endeavors. He was a part of the burgeoning Cotton Kingdom, but in many ways he saw beyond the cotton fields a Florida that could be part of national and international trade, and he had a vision for making that happen.

As a man of status and wealth, Chaires owned one of the premier plantation homes of his era. While this book is an attempt to bring together the very fragmented information remaining in the historical record about Chaires, it is also the story of his plantation, Verdura, and its sad decline from an elegant dwelling house and productive farm to the shadowy ruins of the Old South lost to the Chaires family. Indeed, the ruins, in their disrepair, seem to encapsulate the downfall of antebellum Southern culture.

Ten days before his death, Benjamin Chaires posted a notice in the *Floridian and Advocate* requesting that his name be withdrawn from the list of candidates to the Florida Constitutional Convention to be held later in October in the bay front town of St. Joseph. He had been endorsed for the post by the same paper back in March. He cited personal business affairs that required his attention as the reason for his withdrawal. A day later, in the same newspaper, he announced that as an assignee of Lake Wimico & St. Joseph Canal & Railroad, he intended to sell unused canal land on October 5th. This notification was Benjamin Chaires's final public communication, but his name continued to stoke the imagination of following generations, and his reputation and significance to the history of north Florida were to be of great interest to Floridians for many decades after his demise.

CHAPTER 1
Maryland, North Carolina and Georgia

Benjamin Chaires, later known as "Florida's First Millionaire," was born to Joseph Chaires and Mary Green in Onslow County, North Carolina, on January 25, 1786, not long after their move from Maryland. Joseph had been married previously to Catherine Godwin who was the mother of Benjamin's older half-brother Joseph Scott, probably born in 1784, the same year as Catherine's death. Joseph then married Mary Green (born in Onslow County in 1761) in 1785; a year later she gave birth to Benjamin and then, in Georgia, to Green Hill in 1790, to Thomas Peter in 1797, and to a daughter Mary in 1801. (Another son, Charles Moore, is mentioned in a later document, but his birth date and place of birth remain a mystery.) Additionally, father Joseph Chaires was guardian of a minor by the name of Nathaniel Wright.

*Portrait purported to be of Benjamin
Chaires, from the collection of
James B. Johnson.*

Members of the Chaires family were descendants of French Huguenots and their earliest French immigrant ancestor was Jan de la Chare, born in Rouen, Seine-Maritime, Haute-Normandie, France in 1625. In America, he was also known as John Chaires and was a cooper who resided on Maryland's Eastern Shore beginning around 1666. De la Chare's son, John Charles Chaires, born in 1668, and his grandson, Joseph C. Chaires, born in 1693, remained in Talbot and Queen Anne's counties, Maryland, for their entire lives. Benjamin's father Joseph, a Revolutionary War soldier, and his uncle Charles, both sons of Joseph C., moved from Maryland to Onslow County, North Carolina sometime after 1784. Charles died there around 1787, not long before Joseph moved his wife Mary Green and sons Joseph Scott, Benjamin, and possibly Charles Moore to Georgia.

The pronunciation of the Chaires name appears to have become Americanized over the years. Their original French name, de la Chare, would have been pronounced "duh la Shar." In America, Jan de la Chare used the name John Chaires, but may have retained the French pronunciation "Shar" for his last name. Later, in Florida, when Daniel Wiggins toured the area in 1839, he referred to the Verdura plantation as belonging to "Mr. Ben [S]hears heirs." He also wrote of the Indian massacre perpetrated on the family of Green Hill "Shears," and he used that spelling repeatedly. This may indicate that a quasi-French pronunciation was still used at that time. As a newcomer, Wiggins probably wrote the name the way he heard it from Leon County residents, and would not necessarily have known about the Americanized spelling of Chaires.

Like many other settlers of that era, Benjamin's father may have been drawn to the cheap and fertile lands of the Oconee River in Central Georgia, a frontier that opened after the settling of the Savannah River Basin prior to and after the Revolutionary War. They moved to Louisville, Georgia, in Jefferson County sometime prior to 1790. On December 13, 1807, Benjamin's mother Mary Green died. Benjamin's father, who evidently owned a law firm in Marion County that was dissolved in 1819,

2

died in 1821. By that time, Benjamin was already investing in East Florida land and was making a name for himself in central Georgia and along the Georgia coast.

Nineteenth century photo of downtown Louisville, Georgia, showing the Slave Market built in 1758. Photo courtesy of the University of Georgia, Virtual Vault.

Benjamin married Sarah Powell on February 8, 1811, in Milledgeville, and, by 1821, the first four of their children had been born in Georgia; six more would be born in Florida. His half-brother Joseph Scott died in 1816 in Laurens County, Georgia, and Ben and his brother Green served as executors of their brother's estate at Chaires Mills. The fate of their other brother Charles Moore and sister Mary are unknown, although in January 1806, a deed was recorded for Charles and his father for 148 acres in Jefferson County. Benjamin, and younger brothers Green Hill and Thomas Peter, eventually made their way to Leon County, Florida, where they were to establish new plantations of their own.

The Chaires family arrived in central Georgia at a time of great change. Land was being acquired from the restive Creek Indians, the American Revolution was recently over, and decisions as to the location of the state capital were in the forefront of political discourse. Savannah was at first a logical choice with prime river access and its Atlantic port a boon for travelers and cotton barons alike, but it was considered too far from the now more centrally located population in the new state, so for a time Savannah rotated with Augusta as capital. In 1796, however, Louisville in Jefferson County became the new seat of power. Joseph must have carried some political weight as his home is recorded in 1795 as having been used by the State Legislature of Georgia, as well as by officials of Jefferson County, as a meeting place prior to the completion of state buildings begun in 1795.

Benjamin's early education was probably in the home—he was either taught lessons by family members or by a teacher hired to live with the family. Later, he may have gone to a "learning academy" in or near his home town. There was such a school in Louisville, the Louisville Academy, established by the Georgia General Assembly in 1795, and, as early as 1804 advertised in the Louisville *Gazette* for "a teacher of good moral character to teach reading, writing, arithmetic, English grammar, Latin and Greek." Academies were also established in nearby Eatonville, Milledgeville, and Augusta between 1808 and 1815.

Benjamin was clearly well-educated and was highly articulate, plus he wrote with a beautiful hand. As an adult, he was often engaged in legal matters so it could be assumed that he studied the law, either with his father in his firm or independently. His practice of buying and selling large parcels of land and participating in public affairs had their roots in Georgia during his early adulthood. As he matured, his interests grew: agriculture, banking, railroads, politics, and technology, for which he would have needed a strong background in letters and numbers. By all appearances he was well prepared for a life of influence in many spheres, a life for which he was destined.

The Jefferson County Tax Digest of 1796 reveals that Benjamin's father Joseph was the owner of two slaves and 150 acres of land near the head of the Ogeechy [sic] River and West Dry Creek. By 1806, Joseph's slave holdings increased to 13 on as much as 1,151 acres of land, after which Joseph disappears from the tax rolls. In June of 1798, Joseph was a grantee, along with two others, of 42 acres in Jefferson County. Citizens were eligible to participate in the Georgia Land Lotteries once they established residency in Jefferson County for one year and were married and/or had at least one child. Benjamin and Joseph, as heads of households, were entitled to one draw in the lottery, and were awarded land lots in 1805. In 1807, Benjamin and Joseph again registered for the Land Lottery, but were not fortunate drawers due to the fact that they had successfully drawn previously. Citizens were allowed only one win in the lottery. Strangely, Benjamin was awarded four land grants by the State of Georgia on June 20, 1807, for a total of 441 acres in Laurens County. He also seems to have been awarded three land lots totaling 396 acres in the 1807 lottery in Pulaski County. (Sources differ as to whether the residency requirement was for one or two years and whether citizens were allowed one or two draws in a given year. It is also unclear as to the total amount of land that would be granted in a single draw. In Wilkinson County a land lot [LL] was 202 $^{1/2}$ acres. Requirements and policies may have differed from county to county.)

In 1808, Benjamin served as a witness for that year's lottery, and that year Joseph's name appears on a list of those owing taxes for 1800 through 1807 in Jefferson County; Joseph's tax debt was $1,622.05$^{1/2}$. (In these public records, it is not specified whether the Joseph referred to is Benjamin's father or his older half-brother.) On January 16, 1808, Benjamin sold 202$^{1/2}$ acres in Wilkinson County (later Laurens County) to one James Alston for $1,000. Also in 1808, on March 9, his father Joseph Chaires conveyed 851 acres of land on the Oconee River and Palmetto Creek in Laurens County for a payment of $5.00 from each of his five sons: Benjamin, Green Hill, Joseph Scott, Tom Peter, and Charles Moore. Joseph also gave to his sons 16 "negroes." The indenture stated that, on Joseph's death, the land and slaves were to be divided equally among the surviving sons. Interestingly, the indenture was inexplicably signed with Joseph's mark, a "plus" symbol (+) rather than a signature. It appears that on March 9th, Benjamin sold 184 and ¾ acres of land to Joseph (probably his brother) for $1,200. This land was in the same district on Palmetto Creek as some of the land their father had conveyed to his five sons the same day.

In Milledgeville, on February 8, 1811, Chaires was married to Sarah Powell and the following December their first child was born, a son, named Joseph. His first daughter, Mary Ann, followed on June 6, 1813, then Green D. on September 1, 1816, and the last child to be born in Georgia, Benjamin, Jr., on February 1, 1821. Later in February of 1811, Benjamin joined with brother Green Hill in selling two slaves, named Charles and Bob, from the estate of Benjamin's father-in-law, Nathan Powell. In November of 1811, Benjamin held an execution against the estate of Daniel Sturges, the late surveyor of Georgia. The levy against his estate required the sale of a newly executed map of the state with the return going to Chaires.

The 1820 U.S. Census places Ben Chaires in Pulaski County, Georgia. Between the years 1812 and 1821, his activities seem to have been primarily in central Georgia with a notable list of land and legal transactions between 1812 and 1821. In 1812, Benjamin sold $202^{1/2}$ acres in Wilkinson County to Jeremiah Brantly for $500. In 1814, property he owned in Laurens County was levied to satisfy a debt he owed to one Samuel Fitzgerald. In 1815, three parcels totaling $326^{1/2}$ acres belonging to his father in Wilkinson County were levied to pay taxes Joseph owed to the State of Georgia. Benjamin sold land in Pulaski County, sued one Hardy Vickers of Pulaski County for $620.86, bought land at a sheriff's sale in Laurens County and was witness to a land sale. He was a plaintiff in litigation in Pulaski County and, in 1817, served on a jury pool in Laurens County. He was on a list of Grand Jurors in Pulaski County in 1818 and continued to buy land in various locations. He sold a lot in the city of Dublin, and although he is on the 1820 federal census as a resident of Pulaski County, his name does not appear on the Georgia tax records for that year; he seemed to be living in Baldwin County in 1818. That year, Chaires joined with brothers Green Hill and Tom Peter in selling land. On June 22, 1819, he was a signatory for the dissolution of his father's law firm. At some point Benjamin Chaires is said to have participated in laying out the town plans for Louisville and Milledgeville, both of which became Georgia state capitals: Louisville from 1796 to 1806 and Milledgeville from 1804 to 1868.

In 1816, half-brother Joseph Scott died at age 32, and his estate was administered by Benjamin and his brother Green Hill Chaires. The brothers had applied for letters of administration for Joseph's estate on January 3rd indicating that Joseph had died intestate. On March 26, an appraisal was made of Joseph's possessions, the value of which was $4,118.56. The brothers then had a sale of Joseph's personal property, "Negroes excepted," at Chaires Mill in Laurens County. The sale had been advertised in the March 20 edition of the Milledgeville *Republican,* which stated that the property consisted of "horses, mules, cattle, hogs, sheep, goats, household and kitchen furniture and plantation tools, besides many other articles too tedious to mention." The sale was for the benefit of the heirs and creditors. Joseph Scott left behind a wife, Mary Fenn, whom he had married on December 25, 1811. Other heirs, if any, remain unknown.

A mill on the Oconee River in Baldwin County, Georgia
http://search. yahoo.com/search?p=
oconee+river+ga&ei=UTF-8&fr=moz35

The 1818 Georgia tax record for Pulaski County indicates that "Benjamin Chaires and Brothers" owned 67 slaves, 3,764 acres of land, town lots worth $1,500.00 and one pleasure carriage. Evidently the owning of large tracts of land in different locales was a pattern established early and continued throughout Benjamin's lifetime. At this time the acreage was in Jefferson and Pulaski counties, but there was much more to come. In March, he ventured into land speculation and slave trading in Florida for the first time. At the end of that year, in Georgia, Chaires bought acreage from Adam Simmons and was still referred to in that transaction as "Benjamin Chaires of Baldwin County."

During a time of increased Indian unrest, the British occupation of Florida giving way to the Second Spanish Period, and the distinct possibility of the United States' acquisition of Florida, Chaires seems to have split his time between Georgia and East Florida. He eventually established a plantation east of Jacksonville on the St. Johns River, in an area known as the Diego Plains. He began to increase his business interests in

Florida in March of 1818 when he, along with James Taylor and lawyer Thomas Fitch, purchased 600 acres of land on Amelia Island, along with 57 slaves, for which they paid $25,000.00. Then, in July of 1818, he and Fitch (whom he may have known in Milledgeville and from whom he either purchased or shared part of the Diego plantation land) negotiated for the purchase of 55 "african [sic] negroe [sic] men, forty one of which are on the plantation of Don Bartolome on St. Pablo Creek, three at Mr. John Andrew's in or near St. Augustine and eleven in the possession of Patrick Lynch, all in the province of East Florida." A crop of corn and provisions for the slaves were to be delivered along with the "negroes" to Savannah from the three East Florida plantations by the end of September for $27,500. The Memorandum of Agreement for that transaction was between Benjamin Chaires / Thomas Fitch and Paul Dupon / G.W. Denton.

In a letter from "Providence, St. Johns" in East Florida on May 10, 1820, Chaires and Fitch divided the "gang" of 57 slaves they had purchased from George Atkinson in 1818. He had previously sold Benjamin the so-called Beach Plantation on Amelia Island, a parcel of some 600 acres. On May 27, Chaires wrote from Savannah to Fitch in St. Mary's, Georgia. The letter included an agreement on the division of the slaves they had purchased: Benjamin would get 32 of them, and he listed them by name. He then states that, "We agree that the same negroes [sic] shall remain at planting at St. Johns and the Beach place on Amelia Island till the present crop is gathered and an equal proportion to remain till the crop is prepared and sent to market." In this letter he also discussed a mortgage he had proposed to a bank, selling their cotton ("32 is the top of the market - upland 17 to 18"), the purchase of goods and the dissolution of some Savannah business firms. He goes on to say, "My present opinion is that I shall go out to explore soon after I get home." Unfortunately he does not say where "home" was nor where he would be exploring, but since the letter refers to two plantations, "the plantings at St. John and the Beach place on Amelia Island,"

9

it might be inferred that he had agricultural interests by then, at least on a part-time basis, in Florida. Why and where was he going to explore? The statement was written within the context of other comments about the difficulties being experienced by some banks and firms in Savannah; it might be interpreted that he intended to look for more lucrative and secure markets in other locations—or he may have been looking to buy more land. Not long before he wrote this letter, on April 24, 1820, the United States government had authorized the Territory of Florida to begin selling public lands. This may have been the carrot that enticed Benjamin Chaires to consider an exploration.

The following court case serves to illustrate Chaires's dual-residence status. In Georgia, in October of 1820, "Benjamin Chaires, Esq. of the County of Pulaski," was appointed as an attorney to protect the property and interests of a minor child named William Thomas Jones also of Pulaski County. The legal proceedings were carried out in Burkes County, Georgia, but the 2,000 acres of land owned by Jones were located at Martin's Creek and the St. Johns River near Jacksonville. In the documents certifying his appointment, Chaires is also referred to as "Benjamin Chaires of the City of St. Augustine in the Territory of Florida."

In 1821, Thomas Fitch, his wife and children all died of Yellow Fever, leaving his estate without an administrator. He and Chaires were business partners who shared the purchase of land and slaves on Amelia Island and at the Diego Plains plantation. Chaires discovered that Robert Butler and Duncan G. Campbell of Georgia became executors even though their residence was in Georgia, and they had no real prior connection with Fitch. They also seemed to have come up with "unknown heirs" who, they contended, were awaiting a share of Fitch's estate. This angered Chaires, as he believed there were no heirs. By 1827, there had been no effort on the part of Butler and Campbell to sell off portions of the estate to pay Fitch's debts, so Chaires took them to court to force payment owed to him in the amount of $1,000. A subpoena ran for four months in the East

Florida *Herald* demanding that Butler and Campbell appear in the St. Johns County Court—even though they lived outside of the jurisdiction of that court.

The following year, Chaires was on the list of Grand Jurors, and a plaintiff in litigation in 1821, and was a witness on a land sale in December—all in Pulaski County. As late as 1822, Benjamin is noted as having business interests in Marion County, Georgia, but in the compilation of abstracts from the Milledgeville-based *Georgia Journal*, Chaires is not mentioned for the years 1824-1827. He was, however, purchasing land in East Florida. On the deed documents he describes himself as a "citizen of the United States and resident of East Florida." In 1828, Chaires sold some land in Laurens County and in the transaction, he is referred to as "Benjamin Chaires of Florida Territory," indicating that he was a resident of Florida. In 1826 and in 1831, however, he was receiving mail in Savannah, indicating at least partial residence still in Georgia.

His residency in central Georgia slowly gave way to his finding new directions on the Georgia coast for his civic endeavors, as well as new opportunities for farming, purchasing slaves, and shipping. He then moved south and turned his attention to East Florida with its fertile coastal plain ripe for the establishment of large plantations, still under the Spanish flag, but soon to become a territory of the United States. A recognizable pattern became established: from East Florida he looked to become the owner of thousands of acres of Middle Florida. While establishing himself there, he looked to purchase 20,000 acres in central Florida. He constantly sought out new lands, new projects, new associates, new political affiliations, and greater wealth. He held on to his past but was *always* looking toward the next venture. His constant movement to the south was typical of the significant migration taking place from the older southern states to Florida in the decades following the War of 1812. This mighty migration was to have major political, economic, demographic, and environmental consequences. There is no question that Chaires was a willing participant in the shift southward of his generation's "New Frontier."

CHAPTER 2
East Florida

By 1822, the year Florida became a territory of the United States and held its first meeting of the Territorial Legislative Council, Chaires seems to have been well-established in Florida. He now owned portions of the Diego Plains plantation consisting of around 4,000 acres and the Beach Plantation at Amelia Island where he eventually owned some 1,200 acres. That year he helped design the layout of the streets of Jacksonville (formerly known as Cowsford), for which he was appointed a county commissioner. Governor William Duval, through the Legislative Council, appointed Chaires County Judge of Duval County for 1823—24, but the act appointing him was later declared null and void by Congress. He was on the January 1st list at the St. Augustine post office as having letters waiting to be picked up.

After being appointed commissioner of the Castle Ward, he was unanimously voted in as President of the Board of Aldermen in St. Augustine on November 4, 1823. His tenure as president ran until January 9, 1824. During that time he presided over the creation of a City Constable for St. Augustine, and he combined the duties of the City Treasurer and Tax Collector with those of the Clerk of the Board of Aldermen. He repealed a previous "hog ordinance," and replaced it with a stricter version that made it illegal for hogs to run free through the city streets, and another ordinance was put into effect that required sellers of meat to sell only from public stalls in the public market.

Chaires was included in a list of nominees for appointment to the Territorial Legislative Council by acting Governor William Grafton Delaney Worthington in 1822, and again in 1823 by Territorial Delegate Joseph Hernandez. Also in 1823, he was one of 52 self-identified planters who signed a petition to have the taxes and ordinances imposed by the new Legislative Council on the inhabitants of East Florida suspended. In 1823, his fifth child, Furman, was born in St. Augustine, indicating that the family had by then moved to East Florida along with him; his second daughter, Sara Jane, was born in Jacksonville in December of 1825. In April of 1825, he purchased 125 acres of land at the head of the North River (which may have adjoined the Diego Plains property) adding to his purchase of 500 acres in Cabbage Swamp in 1822 and to which he added another 510 Cabbage Swamp acres in 1828. He also bought a town lot within the City of St. Augustine that bordered on another parcel he already owned, both of which included buildings. In 1825, Chaires conveyed land, which had been previously conveyed to him and Francis Ross by John Brady at a value of $15.00, at the northeast corner of Forsyth and Market Streets in Jacksonville, for what would become the Duval County Courthouse. These three men, Chaires, Ross and Brady, were early settlers in St. Johns County and served as commissioners who oversaw the layout of Jacksonville's streets.

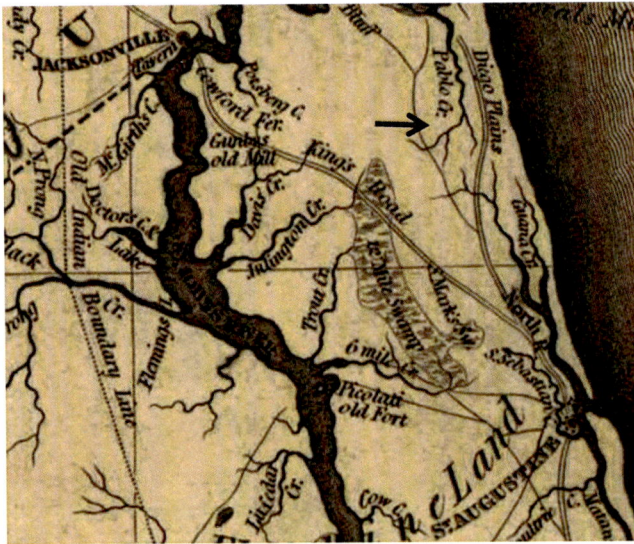

Detail of 1823 map of Florida showing the Diego Plains area, east of Jacksonville.
Map courtesy of the Library of Congress Geography and Map Division, catalog number 2003627045.

14

Florida Indians

Along with the intense migration of Europeans from points north came their African slaves, brought to help clear the fields and build homes and dependencies for new plantations. In many instances runaway slaves sought protection and safety with various Indian tribes. This often brought the wrath of white slave owners down on the Indians and caused them much additional havoc. Records show that time and again slave owners and government officials prevailed upon the Indians to either surrender runaway slaves or to help them in capturing slaves within the Indian lands for the purpose of returning them to their owners. To add insult to injury, some Indian tribes were learning how to farm and successfully create plantations of their own. Even though various state governments and the federal government insisted that the Indian tribes should acculturate into white society, in reality it would have been disastrous for whites because that acculturation would have mitigated their ability to seize Indian lands. This, along with the loss of runaway slaves, eventually reached an unacceptable level of frustration for white plantation owners. They appealed to the United States government for relief. The result was an increased level of resistance and violence on both sides, which led to Andrew Jackson's 1818 "invasion of Florida," signaling the first of the three Seminole Wars.

Although in 1818 Chaires was not yet a full-time resident of Spanish Florida (he was still doing business in Georgia, and his family had not yet moved to St. Augustine), he certainly felt the impact of the situation on his newly formed East Florida plantations. It soon became obvious that the restrictions imposed on the Indians in an effort to thwart collusion with runaway slaves were not working. After the Spanish government relinquished its hold on East Florida, one of the first orders of business for the new territorial Legislative Council was to devise a way to contain the Indians physically on the landscape.

On September 18, 1823, the United States signed the Treaty of Moultrie Creek with the Seminole Indians, which essentially took away all of their lands in the Florida Territory, with the exception of the lands specified for them in the document. The reservation was comprised of land in the middle of the Florida peninsula from south of Ocala to a line just north of Port Charlotte. The east and west boundaries were well inland from both coasts (could not be closer than 15 miles), to prevent contact with traders from Cuba and runaway slaves headed for the Bahamas. Much of the land within the reservation was swampy and not conducive to farming and ranching, although these methods of sustenance were preferable, as far as the white politicians were concerned, to hunting, fishing, and gathering, as had been customary for the Indians; the Indians were expected to adapt.

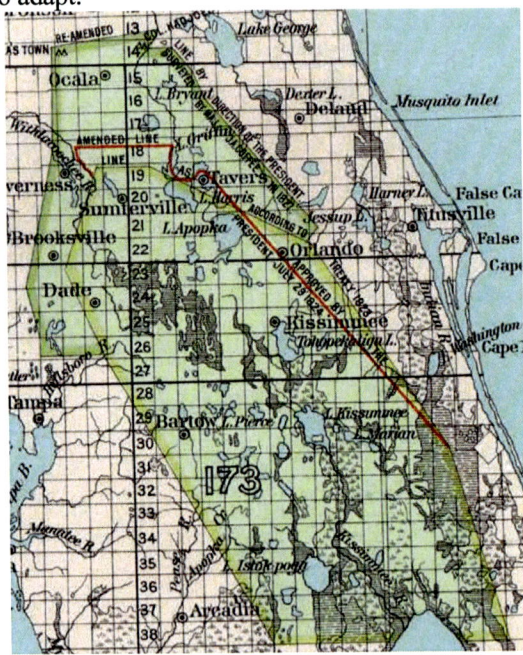

Location of the Florida Indian Reservation in the Treaty of Moultrie Creek, 1823 (yellow) with amendments to the reservation approved in 1825 (red) and 1827 (green).
http://fcit.usf. edu/florida/ maps/nat_am/nat_am03.htm

But, even this act of containment did not work. A comment from a St. Augustine newspaper in 1824 reveals the on-going consternation felt by white immigrant settlers:

> Serious complaints have frequently been made
> by the planters, that their negroes are harboured
> [*sic*] among the Indians with impunity; and it is
> said that many decline settling in the Territory
> because they are liable to the loss of their
> negroes by elopement.

On February 11, 1825, Governor William P. Duval presented a letter from Benjamin Chaires to the out-going Secretary of the War Department, John C. Calhoun, in which Chaires described his views as to the suitability of the lands given to the Indians for farming and raising cattle. He said that he had only traveled through the country two or three times but believed it to be "the poorest part of Florida." He described the inundation of much of the land, the "small light sandy hammocks," which would not bear cultivation but for a few years. His final opinion was that

> the said Indians cannot possibly subsist on their
> present location; and that an extension to the line
> so far as to include the Big Swamp, which is a
> hammock, containing about five or six thousand
> acres of pretty good land, ought to be granted to
> them, which is all asked by them, so far as I
> have heard.

Chaires's testimony may have revealed a more tolerant and empathetic concern for the Indians than many plantation owners. At any rate, his testimony, along with that of Governor Duval's, who expressed a similar but more detailed description of the lands, evidently made an impression on President James Monroe. As one of his final presidential acts, Monroe approved the extension of the Indian lands to the north on February 25th. In the

17

end, the reservation consisted of 4,032,940 acres. Monroe also suggested that Florida's Indian Agent, Gad Humphreys, proceed with finding a site for his agency, which was eventually located at Big Hammock near present day Ocala.

Indian Rations

The Treaty of Moultrie Creek promised that provisions for the "emigrant Florida Indians" would be part of the trade-off for taking away their traditional lands. By order of the Secretary of War, on April 8, 1824, Gad Humphreys sent a solicitation, or request for bids, to the Florida *Herald*, the St. Augustine *Southern Democrat*, and the Pensacola *Gazette*, as well as papers in Charleston and New Orleans; the deadline for the submission of proposals was to be May 30th. The requirements of the contract included supplies of fresh beef, salt and corn or flour in the amount of 2,500 to 3,000 rations per day. The provisions were to be distributed at St. Marks and Tampa Bay within the Indian Boundaries. (This was an odd requirement since St. Marks was nowhere near the Indian lands.) Chaires offered the lowest proposal for eighteen cents and one quarter of a cent for the entire rations, but Duval did not approve it, thinking it was too high a cost. More likely, the rejection had to do with his secret meeting with friends and cronies on the day the contracts were to be issued. Unfortunately for Duval, Chaires found out about this meeting "by accident" and went forthwith to the scene some 30 miles outside of the new territorial capital of Tallahassee to the home of Judge Robinson, a bidder for the contract, where he found that Duval had approved a low bid of fourteen cents per ration offered by Governor Clark of Georgia. Other bidders present included Micajah Crupper and R. Parham. This was not the first time, nor the last, that political favoritism would be a notorious part of the white man's interactions with the Indians.

On May 31st, Chaires mysteriously received word from Agent Humphreys that *his* proposal *had* been accepted, but the contract was not yet ready. Chaires responded:

> I hope the Governor will say, as soon as consistent, to whom the bond shall be given for the fulfillment of it, and the contract formally entered into; until that is done, it will be hazardous for me to purchase cattle, which must be brought from Georgia, or to make the necessary arrangement for the purchase and shipping of corn and salt.

The confusion that ensued over the awarding of the contracts led to another solicitation for bids, this time directly from Duval, to which Chaires replied on July 20. He offered another bid at fifteen cents per ration. He had thought that his bid to Humphreys, which he had been told was approved and accepted, was in force so he had "made extensive purchases of provisions for the fulfilment [*sic*] of said supposed contract, which must inevitably perish on my hands, and considerable loss and injury be sustained by me." He went on to say that he would underbid any other proposal by "one twentieth of a cent less than any other person or persons who may offer good and sufficient security of the fulfilment [*sic*] of the contract." He offered as security John Bellamy, Edward Gibson, John Y. Garey, and Francis I. Ross. He also requested that his contract be only for provisions for Indians located in "East Florida, or on the eastern side of the Suwaney [*sic*] river." He made no mention of the previous solicitation which had included a distribution site at St. Marks.

On July 22nd, Chaires was formally issued a contract for 600 rations per day for the use of the Florida Indians "at or near the military post at Tampa Bay" and he was also to select "the most convenient high ground which can be travelled [*sic*] to from the interior of the country above, at or near the mouth of Oclawaha

19

river, a branch of the St. John's river, as the point where he will issue four hundred rations daily. . . ." Each ration included 1.25 pounds of fresh beef, .75 pound of good salt pork, one quart of corn, one pound of good flour and one quart of salt. He was also to provide buildings to secure the provisions and protect them from the weather. He was to be paid eleven and a half cents for each ration. The provisions were to be given out, beginning the following October 10, for one year on the St. Johns River and for 10 months at Tampa Bay; he would be paid every 60 days if everything went as promised. The contract for the St. Marks site was to go to Micajah Crupper, a friend of Duval's who had a reputation for rather unsavory dealings with the Indians there and who had been present at the "secret meeting."

If all went according to the contract, Chaires was to be paid a total of $18,630.00 for the rations delivered at Tampa Bay, and $16,790 for those at the St. Johns River. Disbursements to the Indians were complete in 1825, and during the first and second quarters of that year, Chaires was paid $24,179.58. During the Second Session of the 19th Congress in 1827, an additional $7,947.59 was appropriated to the Indian Department with which to pay Chaires for his provision of rations for the Indians. He charged the government an additional $1,000 for provisions for the Indians on December 1, 1825, and another $3,000 on October 7, 1828, for stock cattle furnished to the Indians. The furnishing of stock cattle was an attempt to stop Indian depredations and theft of cattle belonging to white settlers; it was not part of the 1823 treaty agreement, but was part of an 1824 Act of Congress to preserve peace on the frontiers. In 1832, there was a balance of $195.00 on Chaires's account owed him by the government for "694 head of stock cattle furnished to Florida Indians in 1825." As late as 1835, Chaires was on the accounting books as having been paid a total of $30,015.96 for rations to Florida Indians.

Throughout the questionable contracting process, Chaires was caught up in his own self-imposed dilemma. Back when Gad Humphreys first sent out his request for proposals, Chaires attempted to bribe a fellow bidder for the Indian provisions contract. He offered to pay one Charles Pindar a sum of $500.00 if he promised not to underbid Chaires. Should Chaires be awarded the contract, Chaires would then pay Pindar the $500.00. Since his initial bid was rejected, Chaires felt that he did not owe Pindar the amount he had promised. Pindar disagreed, saying Chaires was eventually awarded a contract so, therefore, he was still owed the $500.00. When Chaires refused to pay him, Pindar sent his complaint against Chaires, complete with written evidence of the bribe, to Thomas McKenney, the General Superintendent of Indian Affairs. Pindar wanted to prevent Chaires from getting paid by the government while he was still owed the $500.00. Governor Duval then had to answer to McKenney and explain the whole process of awarding the contracts, skillfully skirting his attempt to secretly give contracts to his friends, and defended Chaires as the injured party, not Pindar. Duval's final opinion was that the "business agreement" between Chaires and Pindar was a private matter and did not have anything to do with Chaires's contract with the government. While this was being settled, many Indians died of or suffered from starvation, as the delivery of rations was suspended until Pindar's complaint was resolved. Concurrent with this messy situation, a drought was causing additional miseries for the Indians. Humphreys, feeling sympathy for their plight, loosened the requirements of the treaty and allowed the Indians to wander outside of the treaty boundaries in search of food, and he released additional rations to help alleviate their hunger. Gad Humphreys was relieved of his position as Indian Agent in 1830 and later served as Justice of the Peace in St. Augustine in 1842 and was mayor of St. Augustine from 1852 to 1853.

Allegations against Governor Duval were brought to the attention of President Andrew Jackson in 1833 when he was accused of "malpractice in office with a view to favoritism and his own private interest in the discharge of his duties as superintendent of Indian Affairs in Florida." These charges centered primarily on his secret meeting for the purpose of selectively giving out potentially lucrative contracts. During the investigation of this situation, it was determined that Duval left Tallahassee two days prior to June 15—the day the original contracts were to be decided. He informed no one of where he was going. Chaires testified that "it was by accident that he got wind of this strange movement of the governor." The allegations also included many instances of corruption, primarily at the Indian outpost at St. Marks. Mr. Crupper had received funds that were supposed to support the provisioning of the Indians, but went instead to the construction of a store where the Indians were charged exorbitant prices for goods they were supposed to receive free from the U.S. government. Public money was used in the construction of private dwellings and copious amounts of liquor were sold illegally to the Indians. Witnesses testified that Duval frequented St. Marks and was well aware of what was going on but turned a blind eye to the questionable activities of his cronies.

East Florida Lands

On February 22, 1819, the Treaty of Amity Settlement (also known as the Adams-Onis Treaty) was signed, ratified and proclaimed between the King of Spain and the United States. The treaty laid down the agreements between the two countries as to the ceding of the Spanish lands in East and West Florida to the United States. Both countries were bound by the rules found in the articles of the treaty. Article VIII addressed the granting of lands, today known as Spanish Land Grants:

> All the grants of land made before the 24th of January, 1818, by His Catholic Majesty, or by his lawful authorities, in the said territories ceded by His Majesty to the United States, shall be ratified and confirmed to the persons in possession of the lands, to the same extent that the same grants would be valid if the territories

had remained under the dominion of His Catholic Majesty. But the owners in possession of such lands, who, by reason of the recent circumstances of the Spanish nation, and the revolutions in Europe, have been prevented from fulfilling all the conditions of their grants, shall complete them within the terms limited in the same, respectively, from the date of this treaty; in default of which the said grants shall be null and void. All grants made since the said 24th of January, 1818, when the first proposal, on the part of His Catholic Majesty, for the cession of the Floridas [*sic*] was made, are hereby declared and agreed to be null and void.

In 1874, 36 years after Benjamin Chaires's death, John A. Henderson, his grandson-in-law and administrator of his estate, (appointed after the death of the original administrator, his oldest son Joseph), petitioned the 2nd Judicial Circuit Court in Leon County for permission to sell lands from Benjamin's estate located in East Florida. He was granted permission to do so. On May 24th, Henderson contracted with The Tallahassee *Sentinel* to run a seven week advertisement for the sale of the land, the only assets remaining in the estate. These lands constituted thousands of acres, in the counties of Nassau (588 acres), Volusia (4,905 acres) and St. Johns (4,550 acres). (At the time it was also Henderson's intent to sell 1,200 acres in Jackson County.) There is no mention in the petition of Chaires's "Alachua lands," (to be discussed below) probably because they were still under constraints by the court due to a problematic survey. The reason for the sale was that the Chaires descendants, children and grandchildren, still living at that time were not able to pay the property taxes on such large tracts in the aftermath of the Civil War with no enslaved labor. The properties were not cultivated, produced no revenue, and the heirs were not supplied with cash funds with which to pay the taxes.

The Nassau County land included the so-called Beach Plantation located at Breche Hammock on Amelia Island. Three hundred acres of this land were probably transferred to Chaires by Don Bartolome de Castro y Ferrer who was originally granted the property by Governor pro tem Joseph Estrada in July of 1815. Chaires was not in possession of a deed or title to the land at the time that his claim was confirmed in 1828, but the property did remain in his ownership. Chaires was also the confirmed purchaser of another 300 acres on Amelia Island that he bought from William Lawrence, who had been granted the land in 1815.

The Spanish Land Grant documents indicate that Chaires was also the confirmed owner of two parcels of land which were north of a tract owned by James Pelot and totaled 602.57 acres. The distinguishing feature was Willow Pond, which ran from north to south over both parcels; the land included marsh and was bounded by public lands to the north and west and to the east "at the margin of the Atlantic beach." He purchased this property in 1830 and 1831. This land was located on Amelia Island, but there is no specific mention of these lands in the documents of family descendants.

Amelia Island was described as follows by James Grant Forbes during his 1821 travels in Florida:

> South from St. Mary's, is the island of Amelia, more known of late years than any other part of Florida, as well to commercial men as to politicians:—To the former, from the access had to it, during the embargo by the United States, in 1808, and the war of 1812, during which there were generally in port upwards of 150 sail of shipping of all nations and flags, carrying on an immense transit trade, more favourable [sic] to those concerned in it than honorable to the governments under whose auspices it was fostered:—And to the latter, from its contiguity to the United States, and serving as a resort for

24

adventurers of every kind, and for every purposes. . . .From these circumstances arose the town of Fernandina.

The 4,500 acres of Volusia County land were purchased in December 1829 by Chaires from Thomas Butler, administrator of Thomas Fitch's estate. This tract of land was originally granted to Fernando de la Maza Arredondo by East Florida Governor Jose Coppinger and later sold to Fitch. The property is referred to in various Chaires family documents as the "Halifax lands" and was in the vicinity of present day Holly Hill. (As an aside, Chaires named his second youngest son after Thomas Butler and Chaires called the rise on which Verdura is located Thomas Butler Hill.)

The St. Johns property was the 4,995 acres of land at least partially purchased from or shared with Thomas Fitch around 1820 in the Diego Plains area south of Jacksonville, near the North River; it included Pablo Creek and was sometimes referred to as Chacarras or Chicazas (old fields). In addition to the lands purchased from Fitch, Chaires owned 500 acres of the nearby Cabbage Swamp, which he purchased on August 16, 1822, from Robert Andrew, who had received the land via a grant from the Spanish Government in 1793. Chaires bought another 510 acres in Cabbage Swamp on the North River, the survey for which was not approved until 1836. He rounded out his Cabbage Swamp lands with 125 acres on the North River purchased from the grandson of Robert Andrew in 1825.

These lands made a significant impression on Forbes during his Florida trip, as is evident by his observations of the area:

> The land in the neighborhood of Pablo is held in such high estimation, that many productive settlements have been made, and are now making. The plantations of Mr. John Forbes, on which Messrs. Fatio and Fleming now work their hands, and those of Don Bartolo, Messrs.

Fitch & Chairs [*sic*] and Mrs. Baker, are the most conspicuous.

Diego Plains afford the most luxuriant pasture for cattle, which thrive there wonderfully; the mast for hogs is very abundant, and the wild cabbage is found in immense quantities in the adjoining swamp.

The extensive view of meadow, afforded by the open plains, exhibits a vast expanse of perpetual verdure, interspersed with clusters of small copped trees, surrounding cabbage swamps; the sea in front to the east, and an intermediate line of sand hills in the rear, to the west, treat the eye to the most picturesque prospect imaginable.

Two lawsuits

While busying himself with land purchases and political influence around St. Augustine, Chaires found himself in a rather ill-advised circumstance when he leased land on Greenfield Plantation for the years 1819 to 1821. Zephaniah Kingsley and Philip Robert Yonge managed Greenfield for owner, John Fraser, prior to his death. Later they became the executors of Fraser's estate. Greenfield was located at the head of the San Pablo Creek near the Chaires/Fitch Diego Plains place. (The area today is at Atlantic Avenue and Pablo Creek in Jacksonville.) The property was "uncleared and heavily timbered with live oaks, pine, cedar and cypress...of sufficient quality to produce ships for the navy." Evidently, between 1821 and 1825, Chaires, without permission, "girdled, deadened, injured and greatly damaged some two thousand live oak trees and one thousand other trees at Greenfield." The "other" trees included pine, cedar, cypress, peach and apple orchards and other fruit trees. Kingsley and Yonge took Chaires to court and, since they had planned to sell the oak trees to the navy, they accused Chaires of depriving

Fraser's estate of rents and profits. He was also accused of damaging huts and cabins, fences and hedges, and food for mules, sheep and cattle. They sued Chaires for *trespass assumpsit* and demanded restitution of $15,000. He was found guilty. On appeal, Chaires did not dispute the damages he was accused of causing, although he did declare that he and Thomas Fitch had offered to purchase the property, which he seemed to think gave him tacit permission to do with it as he pleased. He acknowledged that he had "walked on the property and encountered encumbrances" that he pushed down to the ground. The encumbrances were described as faggots, earth, soil, manure, and compost. He went on to claim that the statute of limitations of five years since the trees were destroyed had passed, and that the laws of the United States were not in effect at the time of his misdeeds, as Florida was then still under Spanish rule. The court fined him $20,000 in rents, $500 in damages and $66.86 in plaintiff's court costs; the judgment was affirmed on January 3, 1831.

There is some irony that Kingsley and Chaires came together in this fashion. Both were major land and slave owners, although Chaires had not yet achieved the status of wealthiest plantation owner in Florida. Kingsley was to amass 19,500 acres in northeast Florida, while Chaires had accrued over 44,000 in various Florida counties by the time of his death.

Kingsley's views of slavery most certainly did not match those of Chaires. Kingsley held that the economy could work very well with slavery as the main source of labor as long as slaves were well-treated and not subjected to harsh punishments and abuse. He did, however, go to great efforts and expense to have his runaways brought home. Later in his life, however, he seems to have softened, as he declared that he would not go after his own runaways. There is no evidence that Chaires was cruel to his bondsmen, although there are some indications that he had some empathy and consideration for them as human beings. There is considerable primary documentation for Kingsley and much is known about his relationship with Anna Jai, a slave woman he later married and with whom he had children. While it was not unusual for a slave owner to seek out sexual liaisons with his female slaves, there is no evidence that Chaires indulged.

In 1828, Chaires was again in court as a defendant in a suit brought by John McIntosh (a previous owner of Kingsley's Fort George plantation). McIntosh asserted that Chaires had trespassed on and taken possession of 2,000 acres on the St. John's River that belonged to McIntosh via a British title he acquired from John McQueen. The land in question was known as McGirtt's Point on McGirtt Creek, named for Daniel McGirtt, a British Loyalist during the American Revolution who was also a known horse thief who absconded from Maryland to East Florida in the late 1700s. Chaires evidently spent three years clearing and farming the property and also built "improvements" prior to being charged with *trespass ejectment*. On December 28, the jury was not able to find sufficient damages to bring a verdict, but the judge overruled the jury's request for a new trial, found Chaires guilty and stated that McIntosh should regain possession of the land, with Chaires paying $99.79 in court costs.

The next day, Chaires asked to appeal the judgment. During the appeal, John Ashton, Chaires's carpenter and overseer at McGirtt's Point, was interrogated as a witness and his deposition is part of the court record. Ashton revealed that in 1822 he had taken possession of the land at Chaires's direction and took with him all the hands then on the property. Ashton also testified that in November of 1822 McIntosh called for a meeting with Chaires at McGirtt's Point, where he had assembled a contingent of "three white men armed and 10 [*sic*] or twelve negros [*sic*] armed" gathered for the purpose of removing Chaires from possession of McGirtt's Point. Several other men were present at the meeting where, eventually, Chaires and McIntosh worked out signed agreements saying that one would pay the other $1,000 per annum for crops produced only during the time of cultivation. Who paid who would be dependent on the decision of the court as to which of them would finally take possession of the contested property. Ashton testified that McIntosh did not assault Chaires nor did he keep him from leaving the place of the meeting. He did, however, gain the agreements through threat of violence; in a sense, he extorted Chaires into signing the agreement. In court, Chaires, described as a "tenant lessee," was looking to be reimbursed for the improvements he had made on the site. These improvements included a small log dwelling house, a sick house for the slaves, a kitchen, two corn houses, a blacksmith's shop, a gin house, a log cotton house, a frame cotton house with attached shed, a store house, nine log negro houses, two negro houses of inferior quality, a well, and ditching. Chaires had also cleared 300 acres of old fields, cleared 155 acres of new land, built two large wheels for the cotton gins, plus construction of a wharf and ditching for it. The total value of these improvements was $5,822.00. McIntosh saw these improvements as being destructive to his property and wanted Chaires booted off the land. The final disposition of the case was filed on January 30, 1837, when Chaires paid McIntosh an $8,000 cash settlement.

Whether by design or by happenstance, the property in question at McGirtt's Point had been inherited by William Thomas Jones, the minor child for whom Chaires had been assigned his guardian *ad litem* for the protection of Jones's inherited property at Martin's Creek. Whether this was a rationale for Chaires to believe he could have unfettered access to the property remains a mystery.

CHAPTER 3
On to Leon County

When Chaires began exploring in Leon County around 1824 or so, the area around what was to become Tallahassee had seen little human activity after the British and Creek Indians invaded northern Florida in 1704, burned the Spanish missions, and saw the Apalachee Indians and other native groups scatter to parts unknown. But gradually, a population became established, Spain ceded its land to the United States, and a new territory was born. Initially, the Legislative Council for the Territory of Florida was to meet alternately in St. Augustine and Pensacola. But due to impossibly difficult travel conditions in a very primitive North Florida, some council members made the trip to Pensacola for their first meeting in 1822 by boat, sailing around the Florida peninsula and up the Gulf coast, arriving a month late. To make travel easier on themselves, during their second meeting in St. Augustine in 1823, the council passed an act that appointed two commissioners to explore the land between the Ocklockny [*sic*] River on the West and the Suwannee River on the East, to select the most "eligible and convenient situation for the seat of Government for the Territory of Florida." The two, John Lee Williams representing West Florida, and Dr. William H. Simmons from East Florida, recommended the area of Tallahassee that today is known as "The Cascades" as the site for the new territorial capital. This was made official by an Act of Congress on May 24, 1824. Eventually, the original two Florida counties (Escambia and St. Johns) became four: Escambia and Jackson in the West; Duval and St. Johns in the East. Gadsden County was carved from Escambia; Leon carved from Gadsden in 1824 and named for Florida's first Spanish visitor, Ponce de Leon. A Tallahassee land auction in April of 1825 sold off 160 acres of forest land surrounding the capital square, and in May, land outside the city of Tallahassee was put up for sale at a minimum $1.25 per acre. Nothing could have been more irresistible to Benjamin Chaires or to many planters from northern states. A total of only 965 non-Indian souls occupied Leon County in 1825, but the population of Tallahassee and Leon County saw substantial growth in the ensuing years. The Chaires family was to be a significant engine of that growth, and Benjamin Chaires was a force behind the opening of trade in this part of Florida.

Just as Chaires seems to have moved back and forth between Georgia and East Florida in the early 1820s, so he seems to have traveled between East Florida and Middle Florida for several years. He appears to have been in Leon County as early as 1824, when he wrote to Gad Humphreys from Tallahassee concerning his contract to provide Indian rations, but he was not living in Leon County when the 1825 census was taken. There is, however, an entry which reads "Lawther, B. for Chairs [*sic*]" who was in town with 18 slaves. Whether the "Chairs" is Benjamin or one of his brothers is impossible to determine, but it is certain that there was "a Chaires presence" in Leon County from 1824 on. In addition to the arrival of Benjamin and brothers Green Hill and Tom Peter, the contribution to the growth of Tallahassee included the last four of Benjamin's ten children: Martha, born in 1827; Thomas Butler, born in 1828; Charles Powell, born in 1830; and Josephine, born in 1832. Benjamin Chaires became one of Leon County's most prominent citizens. In addition to being one of the county's largest land and slave owners, he was active in establishing banks and railroads, he was a well-known brick maker, he was a leader in civic organizations, and he was influential in local and territorial politics, all the while keeping his eye on his interests in East Florida.

The Nucleus—The Saints

Middle Florida politics was very much a marriage of the burgeoning railroad industry, the establishment of banks, and land speculation fueled by lucrative contracts given out by the United States government. Chaires, along with others of his status, was prominently involved in all. A loose alliance of political protégés of Andrew Jackson's, called "The Nucleus" and headed up in Tallahassee by Richard Keith Call, diligently saw to it that the wealth to be gained from these enterprises profited the select group, which included a powerful faction of well-known Floridians of the day: George T. Ward, James D. Westcott, James Gadsden, Dr. Joseph Braden, Leslie A. Thompson, Prince Achille Murat, John Bellamy, and Benjamin Chaires, among others. While some members of The Nucleus achieved fame, at least locally, they all showed similar characteristics: they were educated, well-off financially and desirous of additional wealth. They found satisfaction in "playing the game" of politics, government, and land speculation, and they aspired to power. As part of this group, Middle Florida planters and their allies were led to great financial rewards as they created Florida's first political machine. (A quick look at the relationship of some of these known members reveals the politically and socially incestuous nature of The Nucleus: Virginia Braden, formerly Virginia Ward, daughter of George T. Ward and Sarah Jane Chaires (Benjamin's second daughter), was married to Dr. Joseph Braden, a prominent citizen of Tallahassee, whose brother Hector was a director of Tallahassee's Union Bank chartered in 1833; Chaires was founder and president of the Central Bank chartered in 1832.) It was said at the time that the Board of Directors of the Union Bank, which ultimately absorbed the Central Bank, "read almost like a roster of The Nucleus membership."

To underscore the dubious practice of patronage in early Tallahassee, a rather blatant advertisement appeared in the Pensacola *Gazette* in May of 1826 for the newly opened Florida Land Agency headed up by one R.C. Allen in Tallahassee. It was established for "the sale of government and private properties and to complete or adjust land claims, to the benefit of early settlers in Florida." References for this agency were described as "those with special information regarding the quality and extent of the most valuable lands" and included Benjamin Chaires, William Duval, Robert Butler, James Gadsden, Richard Keith Call, and Judge Jonathan Robinson of Gadsden County. In spite of the favoritism demonstrated by the acquisition of choice lands by those "in the know," an advertisement for the sale of public lands in north Florida ran in the *City Gazette* in Charleston, South Carolina, 37 times, from 1826 to 1828, in an effort to attract land buyers to the area.

The political wheel moved like this: a group of investors would go before the Legislative Council and request an enactment for the incorporation of a bank or railroad. The council would approve the act, and the Territory would issue bonds to be purchased by subscription as shares, which would benefit the corporation. Shareholders could then borrow from the bank up to 2/3 of their stock value and secure loans with a twenty-year mortgage. Of course, the shareholders were often prominent members of The Nucleus. Another avenue of influence was in the use of patronage in the federal land office in Tallahassee, which allowed those with "inside" knowledge of the quality of lands to purchase the best and most valuable lands for development and planting. Richard Keith Call actually left Congress and returned to Tallahassee to join the Tallahassee Government Land Office where he "aided in the selection and purchase of choice lands." He eventually amassed land holdings of 8,754 acres and 640 acres where he built The Grove, his princely mansion just north of downtown Tallahassee. Those with lucrative government contracts, such as for providing Indian rations, often used their profits for the purchase of large tracts of land and slaves, which they later used as collateral to obtain additional long term loans or mortgages from the bank. This practice was particularly cruel for slave families who may have unwittingly been caught up in the financial negotiations of their owners. If they were used as mortgages or collateral and their owners had to sell their property, the slaves were often left to the mercy of fate.

In January of 1824, there appeared in the Pensacola *Gazette* a solicitation for the patronage of a new newspaper to be called the Florida *Intelligencer* (later known as the Florida *Advocate* with Leslie A. Thompson as editor). The paper was to be "a vehicle of local and general information, and accessible to all persons who may be desirous of discussing topics of a public nature, or of communicating scientific researches and literary essays" but "personal and invidious disputation, every diversity of attack on private character shall be suppressed." The new paper was to be printed in Tallahassee. A few years later, this paper was described as "a vehicle of abuse and filth and the organ of land speculators and political mercenaries." In 1829, the paper failed and the editor of *The Floridian* was then approached about using his paper as a vehicle in support of The Nucleus; he refused. The peak of The Nucleus's power was in the early 1830s when Andrew Jackson's influence was the strongest, but the year 1833 was the last time The Nucleus was able to act as a political force with any semblance of unity.

A similar group of businessmen became interested in forming a railroad corporation in the town of St. Joseph located west of Apalachicola and in an ideal location to compete for the cotton export trade. They were called "The Saints." The Saints operated in much the same way as The Nucleus and no doubt there was some overlap of membership. A rivalry between the towns of Apalachicola and St. Joseph ensued, but The Saints, with their wealth and influence, were not necessarily highly respected. From the Apalachicola *Gazette*:

> Rumor that the merchants were moving to St. Joseph's Bay is without foundation. That place exists only in name and in the mind of the small band of speculators, who would build a city at the public expense, could they dupe the people by their arts and untiring zeal. But it is a bad cause, a very bad cause that requires such means as they resort to for support.

Chaires's many business interests were intermingled and, indeed, being a player in Florida politics at that time required diversity: land speculating, farming, banking, and railroads, along with legal work, civic organizations and a polished reputation. His involvement with the early banks of Leon County no doubt afforded him beneficial interactions with other wealthy planters and businessmen on whom he could exert influence. Chaires was very active in the establishment of early railroads of the area. He was often one of a group going before the Legislative Council to request incorporations for railroad or canal companies. The banks were involved by providing bonds as "start-up" funds, which were to be repaid through selling subscriptions for shares in the company. Frequently, those who were requesting legislative enactments were the same men who later became directors or presidents of the companies. In addition to the political relationships developed through these business "deals," those on the inside also received perks from the banks on loans and mortgages, along with reduced fees to use the rail in shipping their crops to distant markets. Chaires was part of a banking establishment that often "looked the other way" when mortgage payments came due, which certainly provided him an assist in maintaining his position as one of Florida's wealthiest residents.

CHAPTER 4
The Benjamin Chaires Resumé

Wealthiest Planter in Florida / Florida's First Millionaire

Much has been made over the years about Chaires being the wealthiest Florida plantation owner and Florida's first millionaire, and there is no doubt that he was a wealthy man even by today's standards. But, actual evidence of his being Florida's first millionaire is scarce. Many early bank records were destroyed following the Panic of 1837 to spare embarrassment to families associated with serious financial breakdowns caused by dubious banking practices. Bank records may not have told the whole story at any rate. During that period they served more as vehicles for moving funds to and from various outside interests rather than as repositories of the saved or invested monies of specific individuals. Edward Baptist, in *Creating an Old South*, does not list Chaires with other wealthy land speculators David Thomas, Robert W. Williams, R. C. Allen, and G. K. Walker, who began accumulating wealth by administering the survey of government lands around Leon County. By 1830, they were among the richest men in Middle Florida.

There are a few insights into the cash in Chaires's wallet, however. It is known that Chaires paid $25,000 in cash and mortgaged another $25,000 when he purchased Fauntleroy Plantation. In 1842 (after Chaires's death), a sale of slaves was held, the income from which was to help pay off the mortgage on that purchase. He made at least $30,000 for his efforts at providing rations for the Seminole Indians, and he was paid for his brick- making projects. Chaires left $10,000 to his daughter Mary Ann in lieu of land, which he kept from her so that her estranged husband, William Burgess, would not have access to it. His will does state that he wanted his wife to have his "personal estate" throughout her life, but an amount is not indicated. He willed only land to nine of his children. Because of Chaires's status in The Nucleus, he had access to methods that would have given him a step up in gaining wealth. Deed records show some payments in cash, some in loans or mortgages, and some in slaves. He may have been "land rich and cash poor," but given the lack of specific documentary evidence about his monetary accounts, we may never know his true financial status.

It is doubtful, though, that Chaires would have been the only millionaire in Florida. In addition to the group noted above, there were many planters in nearby Gadsden, Jefferson and Jackson counties who were willing to "play The Nucleus-type game" with land offices, banks, and politics, and they grew rich because of it. It is not an exaggeration to believe there may have been several millionaires in Florida by the 1830s. At any rate, in the antebellum South, a person's net worth was more dependent on land holdings and slave ownership than cash-on-hand, and Mr. Chaires certainly had an abundance of both.

Major Land Holder

While there may not be much available data revealing Chaires's monetary status, the situation is the opposite regarding his prodigious land holdings. In 1826, Benjamin Chaires began buying vast amounts of land in Middle Florida. The records of the Tallahassee and Newnansville General Land Office list fifty-six purchases in Jefferson, Jackson, Hamilton, Gadsden, and Leon counties mostly in the years 1826 and 1827, with additional purchases between 1828 and 1830, and at least one as late as 1835. Thirty of these transactions were in Leon County. There are eighteen deeds in the Leon County archives for private land transactions by Benjamin Chaires between the years 1827 and 1839. By contrast, between 1827 and 1836, brother Green Hill purchased only twelve parcels through the land office, and, his brother Tom Peter purchased only ten between 1826 and 1833. Green Hill purchased fourteen parcels in Leon County and sold five while Tom Peter purchased seven and sold five. (In

1828, while amassing land in Leon County, Chaires purchased 354 acres in Wilkinson County, Georgia, and an additional 50 acres in what became Laurens County.) At the time of Chaires's death, he owned nearly 10,000 acres in Leon County alone, most of which were located in the southeastern part of the county. He owned whole sections or parts of sections in Township 1 South, Range 2 East (T1S, R2E), Township 1 South, Range 1 East (T1S, R1E) and smaller parcels in Township 1 North, Range 2 East (T1N, R2E). He purchased two parcels of what was to become part of his Verdura plantation in 1826, and a third, the parcel where the mansion was to be constructed, in 1827. These purchases were all made when the United States offered up public lands for sale at around $1.25 per acre. If that was the cost of the acreage he bought from the government, he paid in the neighborhood of $3,796.25 for some 3,037 acres. Chaires also purchased lands privately from individuals that included town lots, additional parcels at Verdura, another plantation along the Old St. Augustine Road, and outlying land. One notable purchase was of 120 acres of the "Walton Lands," which had been conveyed to the Territory by the wife of George Walton for damages against the territory. The property, located in T1S, R1E, the center of which today is known as Cross Creek, was divided into lots of 40 acres each, which were auctioned off on April 7, 1829; Chaires bought three lots.

Also in 1829, Chaires entered into the purchase of lands formerly granted to Don Jose de la Maza Arredondo by the Governor of East Florida, by way of the King of Spain, some 20,000 acres in central Florida near the current city of Ocala. The transaction was to have a long and storied slog through the courts of the United States and of the eastern district of Florida before a settlement was reached. The following is a history of the issues surrounding the grant for the Alachua lands as it specifically related to Benjamin Chaires and his estate.

The Controversy over the Alachua Lands

On May 23, 1828, the U.S. Congress passed an act, based on a precedent set for the State of Missouri and the Territory of Arkansas, under which claimants to U.S. lands would be allowed to "institute proceedings to try the validity of their claims." A year later, on February 16, 1829, Don Francis Fatio, the administrator of the Don Jose de la Maza Arredondo estate conveyed to Chaires, along with partners Pedro Miranda and Gad Humphreys, 20,000 acres as a land grant, which Chaires referred to as his "Alachua Lands." The land in question had been granted to Arredondo, prior to Spain ceding the lands to the United States, by the Governor of East Florida on behalf of the King of Spain. (This land should not be confused with another grant Arredondo received, which was located in central Florida and contained 289,645 acres; the location of this "Arredondo Grant" is shown on many period maps.) Problems with inaccurate or unverifiable surveying by the Spanish government prior to the acquisition of the Florida Territories by the United States delayed the confirmation of many Spanish grants, which in turn led to many lawsuits against the United States government after the transfer of lands from Spain. Questions concerning whether lands within the grants had been sold by the United States without proper additional surveys to find boundaries of various parcels posed problems, as they were a threat to confirmed land owners, making them too subject to the confusion of these poorly surveyed properties. One of these suits was brought against the United States by Chaires, Humphreys and Miranda that was continued for many years after Chaires's death by his estate. The much anticipated settlement of these continuing court cases is referred to in the wills of two of Chaires's sons:

> Green D.: Instructions in his will of 1882
> include ". . . . if the agents that are now
> attending to the claims, (for land belonging to

my father's estate) before Congress of the United States, be successful and recover said lands or floats or money, I desire. . . ."

Charles Powell: In his will of 1879 he writes, ". . . .I bequeath all my interest in the claim of eighteen thousand acres of land known as the Aredonda [*sic*] Grant that we hold against the United States Government. . . ."

On March 18, 1817, Arredondo, a powerful Spanish merchant, had presented, on his own behalf, to the governor of East Florida, Don Jose Coppinger, a memorial in consideration of his services to the Spanish government made before the cession of the Territory of Florida to the United States. Among other things, Arredondo had "rendered service under arms" to the Spanish king from the commencement of the insurrection of 1812 in St. Augustine and in the town of Fernandina. He had loaned the Royal Exchequer and the city some $14,000 out of his own pocket as a contribution to the "pacification of the province."

Arredondo's request for compensation referred to the so-called Patriot War, which began just before the United States went to war against Great Britain in 1812. It began with an ill-advised invasion of Spanish East Florida by Georgia "patriots," which became the flashpoint of an attempt to wrest the area from the Spaniards for the United States. The so-called Patriots invaded, expecting partisans to assist in the raid. Few sympathizers materialized, official government support dissolved, and an extended guerrilla war ensued. The conflict pitted American adventurers and anti-Spanish partisans against Spanish loyalists and their allies, who included Seminole Indians and escaped slaves.

Arredondo, through his attorney, requested as recompense for his service, a grant in absolute full property, 20,000 acres of lands known as the Alachua lands at about eighty miles distant from this city at a place which is known as Big Hammock about twenty miles from the river Suwanee about sixty miles westward from St. Johns to which number of acres the title of property should now be issued to him. . . .

Two days later, Coppinger agreed that Arredondo should be granted the land as he described it: "I do grant to the aforesaid Don Jose de la Maza Arredondo the twenty thousand acres of land which he solicits at the place which he solicits them. . . ." The acreage was to be surveyed

without prejudice when an opportunity should offer and the tranquility of the province be entirely reestablished and not dreading assaults on the roads from Indians and other banditts [*sic*] who infect them.

On June 21, 1819, Arredondo, through his brother, requested that Andres Burgevin, a known surveyor with proper credentials and qualifications, be assigned to survey the land grant of 20,000 acres Arredondo had received from the King of Spain in 1817. Governor Coppinger agreed to the request and formally appointed Burgevin as the official surveyor on the same day. Burgevin stated under oath that he would exercise his duties "to the best of his knowledge and understanding." He completed his survey and presented the plat and his certification thereof on September 14, 1819. The plat included land situated on both margins of a creek known as Alligator Creek said land commences a little above the head of said creek and embraces an Indian Town distant about eighty miles from the port at Buena Vista and about forty miles to the northwest of Payne's Town.

It should be noted that Burgevin's description is the first and only time Alligator Creek or an Indian Town is mentioned in documents related to the 20,000 acres granted to Arredondo. A map of Florida in 1823 clearly shows Alligator Creek in north Florida approximately in the area of present day Lake City. This map also illustrates the location of the Big Hammock (or sometimes called Big Swamp) not far from the present city of Ocala, and it is the only "Big" hammock on the map.

Big Hammock was a land feature seemingly familiar to most Floridians of the day, as it is referred to in contemporary documents and records; it seems to have been a universally understood name for the well-known landmark. This must have been very confusing to Arredondo, as he had specifically requested a land grant "at Big Hammock or Swamp" in Alachua, and the Governor had said that was the land he would be given. During this time period, Alachua County swept from the north central section of Florida southward with a narrow slice continuing along the Gulf Coast to Port Charlotte, so both the Alligator Creek and the Big Hammock locations could have been considered "Alachua lands."

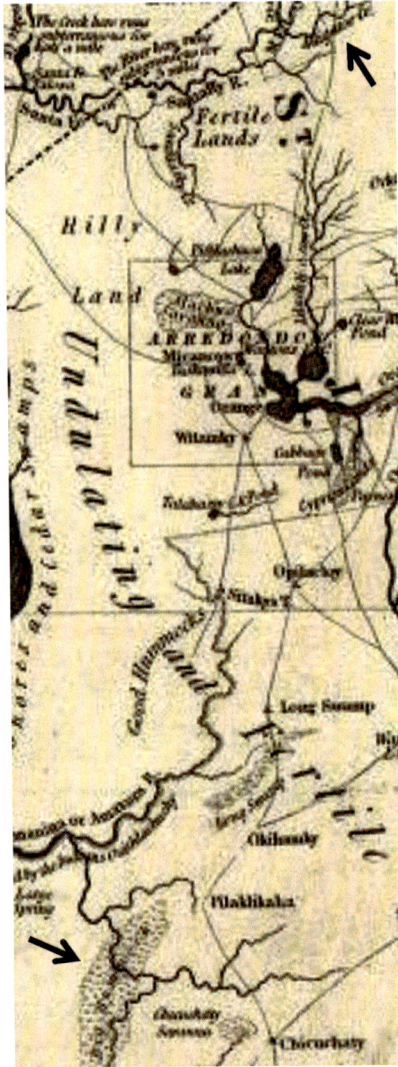

Detail of 1823 Map of Florida showing
Alligator Creek and Big Hammock.
Map courtesy of Library of Congress Geography and Map Division,
Catalog Number 2003627045.

44

In 1824, Congress was mired in attempts to understand and rectify the poorly executed and inaccurate surveys of the Spanish Land Grants. Burgevin was called to testify about the situation some thought was exacerbated by a lack of attention on the part of Surveyor General George J. F. Clarke. On May 20, Burgevin testified that he did go to Alachua but "did not go round the land. I have not been in the Hammock." It was later noted during a Congressional review of the Spanish Land grants in 1835, that Clarke had, "on more than one instance," changed the location of the grants "without the decree of the Governor."

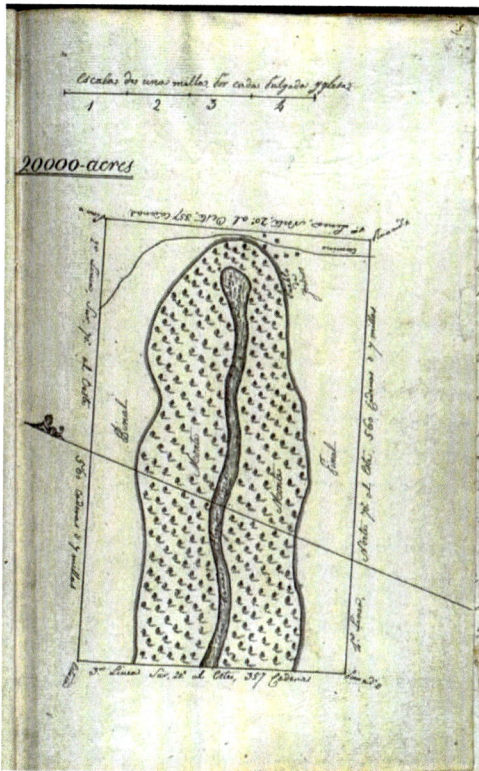

The Burgevin Map of the Alligator Creek acreage.
From Spanish Land grant of J.M. Arredondo,
Alachua and Big Hammock.

In 1824, Arredondo, possibly in response to Burgevin's testimony, recruited the services of Joshua A. Coffee, a known and respected surveyor of Florida lands, to provide him with a survey plat of the lands "in the neighborhood of Fort King containing 20,000 acres more or less called Big Hammock or Big Swamp." Coffee's plat was submitted as evidence along with his affidavit of authenticity during an appeal to the Supreme Court brought by Chaires's estate in 1844. The plat shows a remarkable similarity to a Florida map of 1846 on which are noted Indian towns in corresponding locations as on Coffee's map, as well as paths, roads, and waterways in similar relationships to each other. The 1846 map also shows locations of Big Swamp, Fort King, the Seminole Agency, and Silver Spring. Interestingly, the Coffee map identifies four hammocks, but none are labeled "Big Hammock" or "Big Swamp." He places the "hub" of Indian pathways on the east side of the Ocklawaha River, at the future location of Fort Fowle, established in 1839. Fort King, west of the river, was constructed in 1827 adjacent to the Seminole Indian Agency.

On March 1, 1825, Arredondo sold to Pedro Miranda of Cuba, 4,000 acres of land at Big Hammock or Big Swamp for $6,000. This was part of the 20,000 acres granted to Arredondo in 1817. Three years later, on September 16, Miranda sold one half of his Big Swamp land, 2,000 acres, to Francis Fatio, an attorney who later became administrator of Arredondo's estate, for $3,000. In October, Fatio sold those same two thousand acres to Benjamin Chaires, who by now was a resident of Leon County.

About six months later, on Feb. 16, 1829, Chaires bought from Arredondo's estate for $8,750

> all that tract of land known as Big Swamp or
> Hammock. Lying and being in the County of
> Alachua aforesaid and containing 20,000 acres
> which said tract was granted by Royal Title to
> Joseph M. Arredondo in his life time.

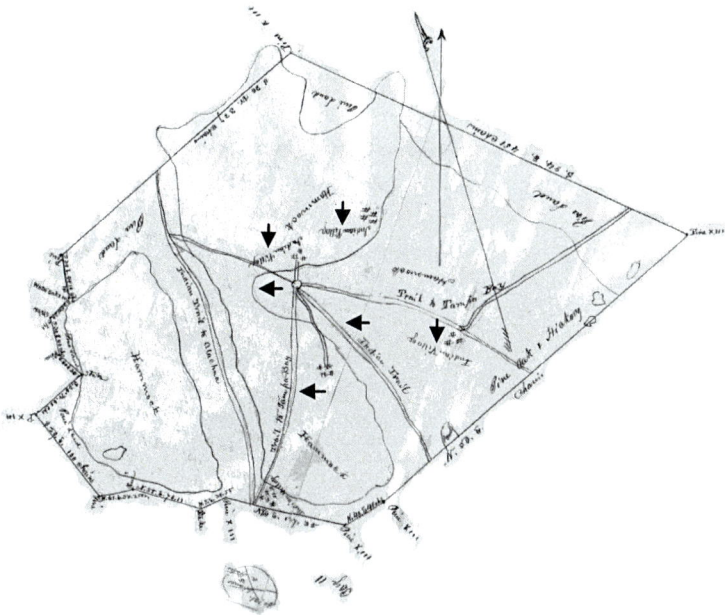

*1824 Joshua Coffee survey map comparing similar features
on detail of 1846 map of Florida shown below.*

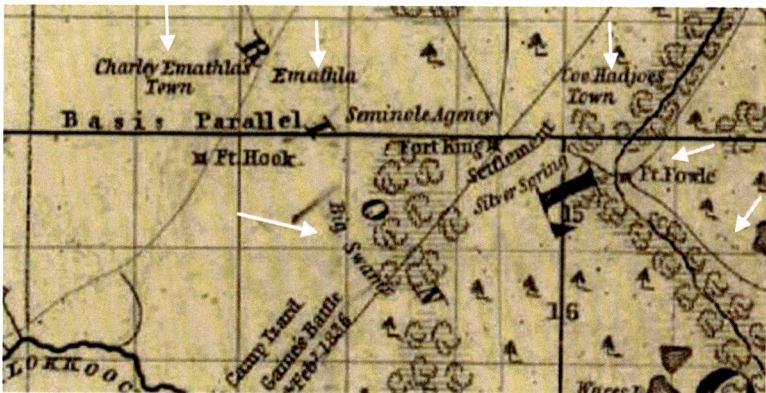

Chaires's interest in the land at Big Hammock may have stemmed from his travels in that area for the purpose of locating an appropriate spot on the Oklawaha River from which to distribute Indian rations. The land was located close to the acreage Chaires had recommended to the Secretary of the War Department in 1825 as suitable for an expansion of the reservation designated in the Treaty of Moultrie Creek. The land he described in his recommendation to extend northward included "about five or six thousand acres of pretty good land." The Chaires deed stipulated the following reservations and exceptions:

> 2,000 acres an undivided portion of the tract aforesaid which belongs to Pedro Miranda and 500 acres also an undivided portion of the same formerly conveyed by Francis Fatio to Gad Humphries, and also 2,000 acres conveyed by the attorneys in fact of Pedro Miranda to Francis Fatio.

It is unclear when Arrendondo began to suspect that the Burgevin survey did not describe the Big Hammock lands he had requested of the Spanish government, or when Chaires became aware of the discrepancies between the Burgevin survey and the deed for 20,000 acres he had purchased from the Arredondo estate. Since Arredondo requested the assistance of surveyor Joshua Coffee in 1824, it could be surmised that he was making an attempt to clarify the issue. In 1829, Chaires brought his concerns to the superior court for the eastern district of Florida where Arredondo's title to the land was confirmed by the judge, and the decree was upheld later by the United States Supreme Court during the January term, 1836. The presentation of petitions to the courts was the initial attempt by Chaires *et al.* to prove ownership of the 20,000 acres: showing that Arredondo had had clear title to the lands in question. This did not, however, prove that Chaires had title to the lands, only that "the [original] title was valid to all the land contained in the survey." Chaires's argument was that he had purchased all the land described in the title from Arredondo's estate, and the Florida court and the Supreme Court later confirmed it. But... where was that land? Was it at Alligator Creek near today's Lake City or was it at Big Hammock in central Florida?

Chaires's land was described as follows (wording is from Burgevin's survey):

> A piece of land which contains 20,000 acres situated on both margins of a creek, known as Alligator Creek, said land commencing a little above the head of said creek and embracing an Indian town, distant about eighty miles from the port of Buena Vista and about forty miles to the northwest of Payne's Town, its first line running north twenty degrees west, three hundred and fifty-seven chains, begins at a pine marked X, and ends at another marked A; the second line running south seventy degrees west, five hundred and sixty chains, and ending at a stake; the third line running south twenty degrees east, three hundred and fifty-seven chains, and ending at a pine marked II; and the fourth line running north seventy degrees east, five hundred and sixty chains.

Confusingly, it was also described as being "about eighty miles distant from this city [St. Augustine] at a place known as Big Hammock, about twenty miles from the River Sawanee [sic] westward, about sixty miles from St. Johns."

On June 27, 1839, almost a year after Chaires's death, a notice to land claimants was announced in St. Augustine by the Board of land commissioners. The announcement proclaimed that Congress, on May 26, 1830, had authorized an attempt to make a final settlement of the Spanish land claims in Florida. All

49

persons holding claims to land under one league square were to file such claims before the Register and Receiver, acting as land commissioners. The lands had to have been confirmed by the Spanish government "subsequent to the 24ᵗʰ of January, 1818." Reports on the land claims were to be sent on to the Secretary of the Treasury and then presented to Congress at its next session. The original documents submitted by claimants can be seen today in the Florida State Archives in the collection entitled Spanish Land Grants. The Arredondo Grant claim was not submitted by the Chaires family, but copies of the documents submitted to the Florida Superior Court in later petitions were filed with claims submitted by the Arredondo family.

Also in 1839, the administrator of Chaires's estate, his oldest son Joseph, ran several notices in the Florida *Herald and Southern Democrat* of St. Augustine, warning the public to avoid coming onto Chaires land for "cutting timber or otherwise trespassing." He describes a total of 4,055 acres at the Diego Plains and Swamp; 600 acres on Amelia Island; 4,500 acres on the River Halifax and another "200 acres held in common with Thos. Butler on the Plains and Swamp of Diego purchased of Juana Llorens." Notably, the Alachua lands were not included in this warning, indicating the estate's concern about the insecure nature of the survey results. They may also have been omitted because Joseph believed the Alachua lands to be located inland, farther west than those along the Atlantic Coast, as were Chaires's other holdings.

Joseph, in an effort to have the Alachua lands resurveyed, appealed to Valentine Conway, Surveyor General of Florida, in 1843. His frustration is palpable in a letter he sent on June 6ᵗʰ:

> The difficulty now arises that no such lands as those set forth in the survey accompanying the decree was to be found, nor any of the lines or marks denoted by the surveyor, nor the stream laid down upon his plat. It further appears that the said supposed survey of Don Andrez [*sic*]

Burgevin does not conform to the description of
the lands granted to Arredondo in the original
grant dated 20th of March 1817.

He goes on to say, "…it is evident, either that the survey of
Burgevin was spurious altogether, or that it was not intended to
denote the lands to which it has been erroneously attached."

Later, in July, Joseph again contacted Conway with the offer
to pay above and beyond the allowable amount per mile, a
surveyor who can complete the work in a reasonable amount of
time if a government surveyor cannot quickly be recruited for the
task. He did not have to hire a surveyor because at some point
within that year, Joseph became aware of the Coffee survey plat.

Chaires's estate went before the Superior Court in Florida in
1844 in an attempt to have the Burgevin survey nullified and
replaced with the survey conducted by Joshua A. Coffee in 1824.
The estate's argument proposed that if Burgevin's survey
conflicted with the land identified in the grant, the "said survey
must yield to and be controlled by the terms of the grant." Joseph
also sent a letter of complaint directly to the surveyor general of
Florida:

> …the said land was duly surveyed and
> admeasured, and a plat thereof made and
> returned to the Honorable Court, and given in
> evidence of said cause, by Joshua A. Coffee, a
> competent and qualified surveyor, but that the
> same was omitted in the transcript of the record
> sent to the Supreme Court. . . .[Both the survey
> plat and Coffee's affidavit are part of the
> original, hand-written transcript of the court
> case.]

The petitioner went on to state that the surveyor general of
Florida would not execute the previous decree of the court [that
affirmed Chaires held the lands identified in the original survey]

unless the decree "shall have been reformed [according to the 1824 survey] by the competent authority [the court]." In June of 1844, the lower court decided that the petition for rehearing could not be entertained and ordered it to be dismissed. In 1844, the estate appealed once again to the Supreme Court, which held that the lower court was correct in dismissing the appeal although it acknowledged that the petitioners were basically snared between the boundaries of the land as it was originally surveyed, the description of the land in the original grant, and the lack of judicial authority to reform the survey. The court held that

> the claimants not being willing to take the land in Burgevin's survey, assumed the right to have a resurvey made, or to have adopted that made by Joshua A. Coffee, on their behalf, in 1834 [the survey was actually done in 1824], which they allege is at the place called for in the grant; and this on the ground that the decree of 1830 is inconsistent, it being a confirmation of the land granted, and also of Burgevin's survey—the places not being the same. This change was refused at the land office here, for the reason that the decree excluded such a change until it was altered by the proper judicial authority. For this purpose the petition for a rehearing was filed seeking to have the decree of 1830 reformed, and that part of it establishing locality and boundaries set aside or disregarded, and the land located elsewhere. This the Superior Court of East Florida had no power to do. . . .

It was then the final opinion of the Supreme Court, as registered in 1845, that the Florida Superior Court's dismissal of the appeal should stand.

So, where exactly were the 20,000 acres claimed by the Chaires estate? The exact parameters of the 20,000 acres at Big Hammock may never be known, although they were described in a Congressional review of the case as being "in a big hammock in the neighbourhood [sic] of Township 15, Range 22 South and East." Indeed, the site of Fort King is within the boundaries of that township and range. The significance of the location may not reside in its placement on a map, however, but rather in the repeated efforts to have the area re-surveyed: it was the belief of both Arredondo and Chaires that the land they wanted, and thought they had acquired, was at the Big Hammock. Had it not been so important to them, why wouldn't they have been satisfied with the Alligator Creek survey? They could have acquired that 20,000 acres and proceeded to do with it as they chose. Previous researchers have postulated that the land was located in Columbia County, in the vicinity of Alligator Creek, near today's Lake City, as indicated on the Burgevin survey plat. The evidence for a more southern location, however, is based on fifty-three years of documents testifying to the ongoing effort of the Chaires estate to have the "correct" area re-surveyed, and the evidence is very much in favor of the location being near Fort King:

- The land at Big Hammock was specifically requested by Arredondo as compensation for his service to the King of Spain.
- The Big Hammock, or Big Swamp, is noted on early Florida maps, was in the area of Fort King, and it was the only Florida swamp so designated.
- Governor Coppinger agreed to grant the land to Arredondo as he described it.
- The landmarks on the Coffee map correspond to landmarks on maps before and after 1824 of the area around today's Ocala.
- Coffee's affidavit states that the area surveyed was "in the neighborhood of Ft. King."

- Deeds for Alachua land purchased by Chaires, Humphries, and Miranda describe the 20,000 acres as being at Big Hammock or Big Swamp, as it was named on period maps.
- No deeds or correspondence or documents were found that indicated Chaires, or Arredondo, had any interest in obtaining land near Alligator Creek.

Burgevin admitted before Congress in 1824 that "I did go to Alachua, but did not go round the land. I have not been in the Hammock." He also related that he had been instructed by the Surveyor General of East Florida, George J.F. Clarke, that it was "unnecessary to make actual surveys." Whether Clarke decided to change the land that Arredondo requested to the lands at Alligator Creek or whether Burgevin got his survey assignments mixed up is anybody's guess. If there had been another grant someone requested for the Alligator Creek area, it should have been easy enough to identify it and to attach Burgevin's survey to it. However the mix-up occurred, the Congressional testimony should have been sufficient for the courts to honor Chaires's petition to use the description of the land in the grant itself rather than reliance on the Burgevin survey map—or they should have allowed the Coffee survey to stand.

Because of the inadequate information contained in the Spanish surveys and the practice of selling off grant land by the U.S. Government, along with the complications of establishing land ownership, justifiable complaints from landowners never ceased. In the early 1880s, the government basically washed its hands of the controversies by vacating the final appeal of Chaires's estate and offering scrip to private landowners (those without confirmed titles) that could be used in exchange for an equal amount of public land offered for sale by the United States. The remaining "unpurchased" tracts were to be considered public lands. In April of 1882, the District Court for the Northern District of Florida approved scrip for 20,000 acres, as claimed by the Chaires estate, which would be receivable in payment for any public lands in Florida offered for public sale. The scrip was issued on November 20, 1883, and John Henderson, administrator of Chaires's estate after Joseph's death, received it a month later. By this time, the three original claimants to the land were deceased and all but one of the heirs in Chaires's will were also deceased; the surviving son was Green D., who died in 1885. Location certificates showing the assignment of the scrip for specific parcels of land are available in the records of the National Archives in Washington, DC.

Land, land and more land

In addition to the Alachua lands, Chaires bought from the federal government 160 acres in Hamilton County, 480 acres in Jefferson County, 400 acres in Gadsden County, and 640 acres in Jackson County. Additionally, there are at least eleven land purchases between the years 1825 and 1831 in St. Johns County; the 1831 purchase being for St. Augustine town lots and three slaves. At the time of his death he owned, had owned, or laid claim to at least the acreage cited below:

Number of Acres		Location
4,995		Diego Plains
1,135		Cabbage Swamp
1,200		Amelia Island
4,500		Halifax River
9,440		Leon County
1,200		Jackson County
160		Hamilton County
480		Jefferson County
400		Gadsden County
20,000		Big Hammock in Alachua County
43,510		Florida Acres

Chaires also owned or had owned town lots in Tallahassee and St. Augustine. The total number, of course, is an approximation and does not include lands he may have retained in Georgia or lands he sold just prior to his death. The total figure merely indicates the extent of his seemingly insatiable desire for owning large tracts of land.

Farmer

Chaires was a cotton planter, which is borne out by his documented efforts to sell cotton at Savannah from his plantation on Amelia Island and shipping his Leon County cotton from St. Marks to ports in New York City and Liverpool, England. He also raised cattle and grew corn for the rations he had provided for the so-called emigrant Indians. In 1834, it was announced in the *Floridian and Advocate* that Chaires was one of three planters ready to ship cotton "at ¾ valuations." At Verdura, in the years following his death, sons Charles Powell and Thomas Butler grew cotton, Indian corn, peas, beans, and sweet potatoes along with raising sheep and cattle. As evidenced by their production of wool and butter, they likely continued an agricultural precedent set by their father. In 1835, the Florida Agricultural Society formed its constitution and Chaires was listed as a member. In 1852, some of his children, no doubt following their father's lead, exhibited horses, mules, bulls, bales of cotton, and Polish ducks during the first Annual Fair of the Leon County Agricultural Society. Son Joseph won a silver cup for the "best one year old filly."

Public documents, such as an annual census or tax records, delineating the output of Florida farmers were not available until the 1850s, and there were no taxes on income from farming during Chaires's lifetime. The earliest tax records indicating the value of cattle were for 1845.

Brick maker

Chaires seems to have been an avid brick manufacturer. He contracted to provide "as many hard burned bricks as may be required under the appropriation for the year 1833" for the arsenal at Mt. Vernon (Chattahoochee), Florida. He was to be paid $9.99 per "M." Chaires and Jesse Willis made bricks for the second capital building in Tallahassee in 1838. Bricks for his mansion and outbuildings at Verdura are said to have been manufactured on site, and the remnants of clay pits can still be seen there. He also may have used the clay bank in the area of the Diffenbaugh Building at Florida State University for bricks needed within the city of Tallahassee, such as in the construction of The Columns. His interest in brick making may have had family roots, as much of the early period of brick building in the colonies in the late 17th century corresponds to the influx of French Huguenot settlers.

The shot tower at the Mount Vernon
(Chattahoochee) Arsenal in 1839.
Courtesy of the State Archives of Florida, Florida Memory,
http://floridamemory.com/items/show/28505

A House Made of Brick: The Columns

Local and family mythology holds that Chaires owned, built, contracted for and/or lived in The Columns—one of Tallahassee's oldest residential structures and present home of the James Madison Institute. The building is currently located at the northwest corner of

Park Avenue and Duval Street, having been moved in 1971 from its original location on the southwest corner of Park Avenue and Adams Street, on Lot #183. Deeds in the Florida Archives show that Lot #183 was originally purchased from Tallahassee Commissioner Turbett Betton by William Williams on November 25, 1829, for $5.00. In an undocumented pamphlet produced by the Leon County Library in 1958, Mary Lamar Davis asserts that The Columns was completed in 1830 or 1831. Unfortunately, she does not indicate her source for this statement. In May of 1833, Williams sold this lot along with some other land to the Central Bank of Florida of which Benjamin Chaires was president. Chaires signed the deed for the property, which included "all improvements and appurtenances and houses." By 1847, the bank was in severe trouble from having provided cash-poor/land-rich planters with too many unsatisfied loans. The lot was then seized by the sheriff and sold at public auction to highest bidders William Bailey and Isaac Mitchell.

The Columns in the 1870s.
Photo courtesy of the State Archives of Florida, Florida Memory,
http://florida memory.com/items/show/10408

It is certainly within the realm of possibility that Chaires provided bricks for The Columns, and he may have contracted for the construction of it. As president of the bank, Chaires may well have used The Columns when he was in town on business, but it is certain from the public documents that he did not own it personally. It is difficult to say whether he lived there while the Verdura mansion was under construction, as some family stories relate. The building of the Verdura mansion probably began around 1829 (within a year or two of the purchase of the Verdura parcels). Indeed, Thomas Brown, on a visit to Tallahassee in 1828 noted that Benjamin Chaires had begun clearing for his plantation Verdura. Since The Columns lot was originally purchased in December of 1829, it would seem more likely that both buildings were under construction at about the same time.

It is unlikely that The Columns could have been completed or even made habitable between December 1829 and 1833 when Chaires signed the deed on behalf of the bank. The family may have lived in or used The Columns at a later date, however. Methodist preacher Joshua Knowles, in a memoir of a trip to Tallahassee in 1836 remembers "the old and spacious Central Bank, a brick building, in which resided Benjamin Chaires and family. . . ." He also mentions that the building was used as a refuge during times of Indian unrest; perhaps the family used the house periodically when seeking the safety of town. Davis, without citation, states that the "Verdura fireplaces are positively known to have been the same structure as these in The Columns, however Verdura was not lived in until January of 1838 [nine months before Chaires's death]." These comments tend to corroborate the notion that the construction of the Verdura house took several years and may indicate that the Chaires did stay in The Columns at some point prior to taking up residence "in the country."

If the Chaires family was not living in The Columns or at Verdura after their arrival in Leon County, where were they living? The federal census taken in 1830 indicates that they were living in Magnolia, Florida, in Leon County on the St. Marks River. (Green Hill Chaires was also living in Magnolia at that time, but Tom Peter

59

does not show up on the 1830 census.) The Town of Magnolia was incorporated in 1828 by the Legislative Council after which efforts were made to populate the area. The town was established for the purpose of shipping goods from Florida to New York and New Orleans, and operated robustly as a port until around 1838, when citizens began to abandon Magnolia in response to the Tallahassee Railroad bypassing the area. A hurricane in 1843 was the final disruption to the river port, and soon thereafter Magnolia was on its way to becoming an "extinct city," as officially designated by the state. Chaires family members continued to own land and do business in Wakulla County until the early 1900s. For example, son Joseph purchased land near Sulphur Springs and his son, Charles Robert, sold his property near today's intersection of Highways 98 and 267 to Ben C. Chaires. In 1850, son Joseph, as president, along with Green Hill and Green D. on the board, were granted the charter for the Plank Road Company for the purpose of building a wooden plank road from Newport to Thomasville. Only a section of the road was completed and a portion of it is still extant as a dirt road from Natural Bridge to Highway 98.

During antebellum times, it was common for wealthy plantation owners, when settling in a new location, to build a small home to accommodate their families while a larger and more impressive house was being built. It is probable that Benjamin Chaires, like other planters of his day, built a modest home as a place for his family to live while awaiting the completion of the more grandiose mansion. In addition to a home in Magnolia, he may have built a small second house, near Verdura, to be used when Chaires was overseeing the construction of the Big House. This house may have been located in the south half of the southeast quarter of Section 18 in Township 1 South, Range 2 East, about a mile north of the construction site of the Verdura mansion; this property came to be known as the Burgess Tract.

Map of Magnolia, Florida from the 1800s.
Courtesy of the State Archives of Florida,
Florida Memory, http://florida memory.com/items/show/
27717

To understand how this hypothesis was developed, it is necessary to move forward in time to 1860 when Chaires's twenty-seven year old grandson, Benjamin Chaires Burgess, died. At the time of his death, Burgess owned and lived on a parcel of land formerly owned by his grandfather on the south half of the southeast quarter of Section 18 in T1S, R2E.

Burgess was the son of Mary Ann Chaires and William G. Burgess. Mary Ann was Benjamin Chaires's oldest daughter, who married Burgess in 1831 when she was 18 and he was 31. Burgess was a businessman in Tallahassee and Thomasville, who was well known as a drinker and charming con artist prone to public misconduct. He had indebted himself financially to many prominent Tallahassee businessmen including his father-in-law, to whom he owed $4,000.00 on a mortgage. Burgess was so disliked by Chaires that he excluded Mary Ann from the same inheritance he provided for her siblings so that Burgess would not receive any benefit therefrom.

Sometime after 1834, Mary Ann separated from Burgess but he evidently continued to cause her so much distress that two of her brothers, Joseph and Green D., went to court on her behalf in 1840 to prevent Burgess from "molesting" her any more. At that time, she was living with "kindred," presumably with Joseph and the rest of the family, probably at Verdura. Perhaps Benjamin Burgess came by his property when his mother's guardians, brother Joseph and uncle Green Hill, "gave" her a former Chaires residence in which to live and raise her son. It would follow then, that if this occurred, Burgess inherited the property after his mother's death in 1845. Later, in 1861, Charles Powell Chaires purchased this property when Burgess's estate was auctioned to pay his debts. Charles Powell's interest in retaining the parcel may have been its importance to the family as an early home.

Railroads, Canals, and Shipping

An early attempt at railroad building occurred in Florida in 1830 when it was requested that Congress fund a survey for a railroad to run between St. Marks and Augusta, Georgia. This effort, however, never came to fruition. In 1831, Florida's first true railroad, for which Chaires was a commissioner, the Leon Rail-Way Company, was approved by the Legislative Council. Its line from Tallahassee to St. Marks was not completed until several years later after it had been re-chartered as the Leon Railroad Company. Its successor, the Tallahassee Railroad, of which Chaires was a charter stockholder, was approved on February 10, 1834, and remained viable into statehood. This railroad was often referred to as "Call's Railroad" after General Richard Keith Call because he owned the controlling stock in the company. Some of the railroad investors donated slave labor in lieu of paying cash for their subscriptions, and at least 50 such bondsmen were working on the line by 1834.

The Tallahassee Railroad Depot.
Drawing by Francis Castlenau, 1838.
Courtesy of the State Archives of Florida, Florida memory,
http://floridamemory.com/items/show/ 25898

63

As early as 1825, pioneers were discussing a ship canal to link the Chipola and Apalachicola rivers with a deep-water harbor at St. Andrews' Bay. A request for incorporation was submitted to the House of Representatives in 1828, and in 1832, the territory's Legislative Council and acting governor James D. Westcott approved "An act to incorporate a company to be called the St. Andrews and Chipola Canal and Rail Road Company." The purpose of the company was to "open a communication, connecting the waters of the Appalachicola [*sic*] and Chipola rivers with the eastern arm of the bay of St. Andrews." Chaires was one of several men who petitioned for the incorporation; others were W.G. Burgess (the much disliked son-in-law of Chaires), Henry Bond, Thomas Brown, and T.R. Betton, who served as superintendents for Tallahassee. Superintendents were also assigned for Marianna, Webbville, and Pensacola. The superintendents were charged with taking subscriptions for stocks to be invested in the new company; Tallahassee was allowed 500 shares to sell. The company was chartered to build a canal or railroad for the purpose of moving goods from the Chipola River to St. Andrews Bay. Later the corporation was called the St. Andrews and Chipola Canal Company. The canal was never constructed, but it signaled the beginning of an interest in facilitating shipping within Middle Florida either by water or by rail.

Chaires's most ambitious railroad/canal effort was the Lake Wimico and St. Joseph Canal and Railroad Company in St. Joseph (today's Port St. Joe). He was president of the company at the time of his death in 1838, and he had been one of the main backers of the proposal for the St. Joseph canal/railroad at its inception, and he was later on its Board of Directors. It was originally requested of the Legislative Council to incorporate a company to be called the Lake Winiico [*sic*] and St. Joseph's Canal Company; the act passed February 11th, 1835. Being a member of the well-heeled "Saints," Chaires had contributed some of the initial $250,000 for the new company and encouraged quick development of the town of St. Joseph. Indeed, prior to the incorporation, Chaires advertised in the *Floridian and Advocate* throughout January and early February 1835 for "hands to work on the railroad."

Residents of Apalachicola were derisive of the attempt to build up St. Joseph, calling it the work of a "few speculators building a town where nature has said there shall be none." Arguments in defense of Apalachicola or St. Joseph as the most appropriate location for access to the river grew more vehement as time went by. Eventually, the Apalachicola *Gazette* listed men in favor of St. Joseph from as far away as New York and Key West. From Tallahassee, St. Joseph proponents included, in addition to Benjamin Chaires, R.K. Call, J.G. Gamble, R. Gamble, John Shepherd, Judge Randall, John Parkhill, Jesse Willis, William Craig, Joe Croskie, Win Wyatt, H.F. Simmons, R.C. Allen, and John Endiman.

A promissory note issued by the Wimico and St. Joseph Canal & Railroad Company, 1837.
Courtesy of the State Archives of Florida, Florida Memory,
http://floridamemory.com/items/show/5737

The company had been originally chartered in 1835 as a canal company to allow the passage of goods from St. Joseph to Columbus Bayou on Lake Wimico, an arm of the Apalachicola. A steamboat wharf was erected there, along with warehouses for storage of cotton bales which awaited further conveyance by steamboat up the Apalachicola River. The canal was never constructed, as the backers decided a railroad would be more desirable. The Lake Wimico firm finally opened for business in March of 1836; it was the first operating rail line in Florida, using mule power to pull the cars from St. Joseph to Lake Wimico. In September, however, a Baldwin locomotive brought over 300 visitors to St. Joseph in twelve cars; this was the first steam powered rail service in Florida. In August of 1836, Chaires delivered a report to the public on behalf of the Board of Directors that painted a very rosy picture of the state of affairs for the new railroad:

> The board of directors of the Lake Wimico and St. Joseph Canal and Rail Road Company, announce for the information of the public, that their Rail Road of a little less than eight miles in length, connecting this port [St. Joseph] with the Apalachicola River, has been completely finished for use—that the company have in readiness on the road a sufficient number of passenger cars, to ensure promptness and dispatch [sic] in the transportation of passengers, merchandise, and produce—that TWO OF BALDWIN'S IMPROVED LOCOMOTIVE ENGINES, have arrived and are in successful operation on the road. Experienced Engineers [sic] and mechanics are in the employ of the company and workshops [sic] have been constructed and complete set of tools obtained.
>
> Ample wharf room and extensive store houses at the Depot, or termination of the road on Bayou Columbus, are ready for use. And the wharf and large warehouses belonging to the company at this place have so far progressed towards

completion, as to leave no doubt of their being finished in a short time.

Chaires went on to say that the Board wanted to be sure all was ready before announcing the completion of the railroad so that business owners could count on it for prompt and accurate transportation. He described the depth of the channel through which the ships will travel as being sufficient. He ended with a curious *non sequitor,* probably a reference to the ongoing rivalry between the towns of Apalachicola and St. Joseph:

> The Directors have been informed that reports have been circulated abroad, by persons who are either ignorant or malicious, that the population of this place were [*sic*] quite sickly, and that the location had proved unhealthy. All such reports are utterly false, and without the shadow of foundation.

With cotton trade being the impetus for the railroad, costs were low for planters: 15¢ per bale. In 1838, the railroad transported some 38,000 bales from St. Joseph to the Columbus Bayou. Problems persisted, however, with clogged channels that hampered the Georgia-bound steamboats' passage from Lake Wimico north, and low water and silt back-up that left steamboats grounded in the mud. The directors of the company decided to move their operation to a site on the main channel of the Apalachicola, to the town of Iola where another wharf was built along with the requisite warehouses.

A $325,000 rebuilding contract was given to Chaires, and the line's name was changed to the St. Joseph and Iola Railroad. Problems continued, however, in the construction of the 28 mile course from St. Joseph to Iola: the need for trestles to be built over the Dead Lakes, a swinging bridge was needed to cross the Chipola River, there was a lack of ready workers, and there were fears of Indian attacks that sent potential workers packing. These setbacks left the company with little cash, so it was forced to use scrip to pay its bills. Chaires refused to be paid in scrip himself and he kept all the company's notes, deeds and mortgages under his control. Work continued, but at a slow pace. In the August 3, 1837, *Floridian and Advocate*, Chaires advertised the need for additional workers: "$30 to $40 per month given to subscribers for Negro Fellows to work on the St. Joseph and Iola RR." He had promised hundreds of workers would finish the line by the fall.

St. Joseph experienced rapid growth, and residents and visitors alike enjoyed the finest accommodations and sumptuous feasts at what today would be called a "tourist destination." The attention brought to St. Joseph made it the perfect location for the Florida Constitutional Convention for which Chaires had been nominated as a delegate. It is evident that part of the "personal private business" he cited as his reason for refusing the nomination to the convention was his commitment to the railroad. High times for St. Joseph, however, were not to last. The railroad, with its new name, finally opened in 1839, but without Chaires's leadership, profits dwindled, and the town of St. Joseph, beset with Yellow Fever outbreaks, several severe hurricanes, and the demise of the railroad, eventually went into decline.

As administrator of his father's estate, Joseph Chaires entered into a suit against the Lake Wimico and St. Joseph Canal and Railroad Company to obtain dividends from monies his father invested as a shareholder of the company. The suit resulted in a public sale conducted by U.S. Marshall Peter Gautier, Jr. of the Apalachicola District on September 1, 1841. Virtually all property belonging to the corporation was up for sale including turn-outs, stations, bridges, warehouses, workshops, wharves, docks, iron, locomotive engines and tenders, freight cars, passenger cars, dirt cars, wagons, carts and mules. The sale also included tools, materials and instruments, along with all land and roads, junctions, and rights of way contiguous to the railroad bed. Prior to his death, Chaires had agreed to exchange stock he owned in the Tallahassee Railroad with stock sold by Richard Keith Call in the St. Joseph Company. Chaires died before the transaction was made and Joseph later transferred to Call the ownership of his father's 441 acres that was to have been part of the Tallahassee Railroad.

Chaires's last public involvement in the transport of goods began on February 11, 1838, when the Legislative Council, along with Governor Call, approved an act that a group of men, seeking incorporation, should be deemed a "body politic." The act also created a corporation called The Florida Steam Packet Association Company of which Benjamin Chaires was a member. The purpose of the company was to transport goods to and from New Orleans and St. Marks, from intermediate ports to St. Marks and from St. Mary's via the St. Johns River. Any serious involvement by Chaires in this endeavor would have been cut short by his death the following October.

Banker

On December 19, 1829, the Legislative Council enacted a law that incorporated the Bank of Florida in Tallahassee. Subscriptions were to open on January 1, 1830, with Chaires as Superintendent for subscriptions. This act also repealed the incorporation of an earlier effort to establish the Bank of Florida on November 23, 1828. The 1829 legislation was the first to be successfully approved and chartered by the Legislative Council after several previous efforts were vetoed by Governor Duval.

In 1832, Chaires became the founder and president of the Central Bank and he also owned stock in the Merchants and Planters Bank of Magnolia, which was chartered that same year. Commissioners for the Central Bank were John Gamble, Richard Keith Call, Benjamin Chaires, George Fauntleroy, T.R. Betton, Robert W. Williams, James McMullin, Richard Hayward and Henry Bond. On May 1, 1833, Chaires signed the deed conveying ownership of Lot 183 in Tallahassee from William Williams to the Central Bank. This was the lot where The

Columns was situated, connected by an outdoor walkway to the small masonry building "around the corner" which housed the bank. The building, now known as the Union Bank Building, has been moved to the south side of Apalachee Parkway within sight of Florida's Historic Capitol. On January 5, 1835, Chaires was one of nine elected to the Board of Directors of the Central Bank. At a subsequent meeting of the Board, he was unanimously re-elected as President.

In January of 1834, allegations about the misappropriation of funds and deceitful practices were the basis of a lawsuit brought against the Magnolia bank by the Central Bank. In light of this, the Legislative Council decreed that a committee should be formed to review the Magnolia Bank's procedures and report its findings. The committee found that on November 12, 1833 the following resolution was adopted:

> *Resolved*, That [*sic*] the President (with the
> Cashier under his direction) constitute a Board
> for the transaction of all business relating to the
> Bank during the absence of a board.

The resolution was signed by Jeremiah Powell who was President of the bank. Powell then promptly resigned his position and Thomas G. Gordon was elected to fill the vacancy. He fulfilled his duties until November 27th, when he left the territory and gave over his responsibilities to the cashier, Edward Seixas, under the following order:

> that the Cashier be a Board for the transaction of
> all business relating to this Bank, during the
> absence of the President, and of the Board of
> Directors.

The review committee acknowledged that this was a blatantly illegal act which also contradicted the bank's charter, but because the Central Bank had already instituted legal proceedings, deemed it unnecessary to recommend any additional measures be taken against the bank.

Twenty dollar note from the Merchants & Planters Bank of Magnolia, dated 1833 signed by Seixas as cashier.
Courtesy of www.williamyoungerman.com

Chaires's Central Bank sued the Magnolia Bank for indebtedness in the amount of $5,542. Chaires and cashier Leslie A. Thompson swore before Justice of the Peace, Turbett R. Betton, the truth of the following allegations brought against the Magnolia bank: "[They] used contrivances and pretenses to enable the defendant and those connected with it, and who have had control and management thereof, to deceive and defraud."

They contended that Thomas G. Gordon and the stock-holders were liable for damages to the Central Bank and to the bank's holders of notes and bills. (In at least one instance, Gordon's slaves were appropriated in lieu of cash payment.) In March, the Magnolia Bank agreed to pay the debts and settled with the Central Bank to everyone's satisfaction, but Chaires requested that Magnolia also pay all court costs, and Magnolia was ordered not to issue any notes until the whole matter was settled. Later that summer, the Magnolia bank brought an injunction against Benjamin Chaires and the other directors, bonding them for $20,000 to be used to pay the "costs, damages,

71

expense and charges" they incurred from the complaint. In the end, the Central Bank recovered its losses, the receivers charged the Magnolia Bank for their expenses, and all papers and documents were returned to both banks.

One outcome of the report offered by the select committee was that the Legislative Council passed an act that required the presidents and cashiers of all banks in the Territory to submit to the Governor "a true and correct statement of all their affairs, under oath on the first Monday of November in each and every year, to be submitted by him to the council." Chaires submitted reports for the years 1835 and 1837, which showed that the incoming and outgoing dollars balanced out at $393,578.80 for 1835 and at $644,440.46 for 1837. The reporting requirement was a well-intentioned effort to provide more oversight of the banks, but the Central Bank eventually failed in 1838, due primarily to the aforementioned questionable practices of The Nucleus, and was eventually absorbed by the Union Bank, which opened for subscriptions in 1837.

The Union Bank Building in the 1870s.
Photo courtesy of the State Archives of Florida, Florida
Memory, http://florida memory.com/ items/show/31817

One of Chaires's responsibilities as president of the bank was as a federal pension agent. He was transferred funds from the government with which to pay Revolutionary War veterans their pensions. He received from the U.S. Treasury $1,000 dollars for distributions in 1836 and $3,328 in 1837. His name was on the books of an auditor transmitting statements to the Comptroller of the Treasury on December 29, 1838, regarding officers whose accounts had not been active within the year. This report showed a balance for Benjamin Chaires of $212 for pensions as of May 16, 1838, "being disbursed." Later, the account was deemed inactive due to Chaires's death in October.

Organizations and Political Activities

- In 1831, Chaires was elected president of the Fellenburg Institute, an organization devoted to the development of agricultural and mechanical education for blacks.
- Although he was never *elected* to public office, by 1832 Chaires had been appointed a Commissioner of Tallahassee, served as Presiding Judge in the Leon County Court, and was nominated to be a Justice of the Peace in Leon County on February 12, 1837, by the Legislative Council, along with 17 others.
- Chaires was nominated to be a delegate at the Constitutional Convention of 1838, but he later withdrew his nomination due to his involvement with private business. At the time, he was heavily committed to the completion of the St. Joseph and Iola Railroad. Ironically, even if he had not withdrawn from consideration as a delegate, he would not have been present at the convention, as he died two months before it convened on December 3, 1838.
- During the years 1826 to 1828, Chaires's name appears in advertisements for the Florida Land Agency as a reference along with William P. Duval, Robert Butler, James Gadsden, Richard Keith Call, and Jonathan Robinson, no doubt members of The Nucleus. Thirty-seven of these ads appeared

in the *City Gazette* of Charleston, showing that there was an intense interest in drawing settlers from other parts of the South to Leon County to buy public lands at very low prices.

- Chaires was active as an executor for estates, most notably for Davis Floyd, his attorney in the McIntosh lawsuit and one-time Treasurer of the Territory. Chaires also frequently served as administrator for his family's estates.
- He provided references for lawyers, such as Hamlin V. Snell, an attorney in Apalachicola, and for academies as far removed as the Bridgeton High School in West Jersey.
- Chaires, as a Trustee, served on the Board of Commissioners for the University of Florida and was active in soliciting an appropriation of funds from the Legislative Council for two townships of land for two "seminaries of learning" each: one east of the Suwannee River and one to the west. These were to become universities when Florida became a state. On May 4, 1836, the Committee on Public Lands approved the request and the act was authorized by Congress for the Governor to purchase the lands. Many years later these academies became the University of Florida in Gainesville and Florida State University in Tallahassee.

There are public documents that often refer to Chaires as "Major" Benjamin Chaires, and some family papers seem to indicate that he received that rank through military service, perhaps in the War of 1812 or the Patriot War. Indeed, a society column in the Tallahassee *Democrat* (date unknown) asserts that Chaires served as "Mounted Gunman" in Georgia and Florida Indian Wars and "figured in conclusions of Chief Micanopy. He was a Major in the War of 1812."

In 1930, a descendant of the Chaires family attempted to find out whether Chaires had indeed participated in the military by inquiring of the Adjutant General's Office regarding service records for anyone named Benjamin Chaires. The answer to his inquiry was sent to the Honorable Tom A. Yon of the House of Representatives. Yon was told that there were no men with the name of Chaires found in volunteer service from Georgia during the years of the War of 1812. It is conceivable that he may have joined a militia, but many Georgia Militia records were destroyed long ago. Further research into this issue yielded no results. There were no pension records found for Chaires and online research of military files revealed no information about Chaires and war time service. Ironically, his son and namesake, Benjamin Chaires, Jr., was also referred to as "Major Chaires" at times, although he did not gain that rank during his participation in the Civil War. His son, Benjamin III (or Ben C.), described his father's military service as follows:

> Called Major Ben but held no office. At one time being in Virginia, he shouldered his musket & tramped through the vally [sic] to repel a raid. Did not belong to the army, but with musket was in the time of battle at Olustee Fla—again at New Port and the Natural Bridge fights in Fla.

CHAPTER 5
Benjamin Chaires and Slavery

Benjamin Chaires was born into a society whose economic underpinnings were based on the benefits of slave labor. It is doubtful that he would have questioned the system of enforced bondage that by the time of his childhood was firmly entrenched in the southern tier of the country. Indeed, he watched his father, Joseph, who, between the years 1799 and 1808, increased his slave holdings from two to 23. By 1818, when he was 32 years old, Benjamin and his brothers Green Hill and Tom Peter shared 67 slaves on land they owned in Jefferson and Pulaski counties in Georgia. In 1820, Chaires owned 68 slaves in Pulaski County.

In 1818, Chaires and lawyer Thomas Fitch negotiated for the purchase of 55 male slaves and provisions for the slaves to be delivered to Savannah from different East Florida plantations. In Providence, St. Johns, in East Florida on May 10, 1820, Chaires and Fitch divided a "gang" of 59 slaves they had purchased from George Atkinson. The following are the slaves listed as Chaires's share of the purchase:

- Old Mary, Old Joe, his wife Nanny and their children Hosea, Moses, Maria, Bob, Isaac and Elsa
- Cain and his wife Little Mary
- Joe Gordon and his wife Cumba and infant David
- July and his wife Long Mary and their children Simon, Judy and Peter
- Ned, a small fellow
- Tom and his wife Louisa and their children Betsy and Daniel
- Jim and his wife Amaritta and their child Pender
- Beauty and his wife Big Nancy
- Edward
- Qua Billy

- Joe ("one of the gang we purchased from McKinnie and Dupon")

The presence of African-Americans at Verdura may have begun with the importation of slaves by Benjamin Chaires in the mid-1820s. The first indication of Chaires-owned slaves in Leon County is in the 1825 Territorial Census wherein Lawther, B. for Chairs [*sic*] possessed 18 slaves. It is not known, however, to which "Chairs" the entry refers. Benjamin's brothers, Green Hill and Tom Peter, may have been present in Leon County at that time.

The number of slaves owned by Benjamin Chaires at Verdura was variable. Tax records show that he claimed 107 slaves for 1829, and the 1830 census shows that he owned 213 slaves: an increase of over 100 slaves in less than a year. There are no tax records available for the years 1830 to 1838. In 1839, the year following his death, Chaires's estate owned 80 slaves, and the census of 1840, in which his oldest son Joseph is the head of the household at Verdura, shows the number of slaves to be 302, with around 235 of them employed in agriculture. There are no occupations listed for the remaining 67, but it is probable that some were used as house servants, cooks, blacksmiths, drivers, and more. Benjamin Chaires certainly used slaves to build his mansion house at Verdura, which would have included numerous construction activities, including clearing the land, cutting and milling of trees for lumber, brick and mortar production for the house and dependencies, wood workers to design and provide railings, stairways, and decorative features, the construction of slave quarters, and for many other building projects in which he was involved.

In addition to the familiar plantation chores attended to by bondsmen of the period, the Chaires slaves are said to have contributed to the construction of the Bellamy Road, later called the St. Augustine Road, and in 1830, Chaires provided slave labor and two drivers "from Magnolia" for the clearing of the channel in the St. Marks River. In January and February of 1835,

Chaires advertised for "persons having able bodied hands for hire," to contact him for available work on the new Tallahassee Railroad. Two years later, he again advertised, this time in a "Notice to Slaveholders," in the August 3, 1837, *Floridian and Advocate*: "$30 to $40 per month given to subscribers for Negro Fellows to work on the St. Joseph and Iola RR." He had assured the public that he had sent "upwards of 150 negro labourers [*sic*] to work upon [the railroad]." He also anticipated having "several hundred" additional hands engaged in a few weeks so the line would be finished by the fall.

Chaires bought and sold slaves regularly in Georgia and in East and Middle Florida. In 1831, he purchased a house lot in St. Augustine from Squire Streeter and wife that included a slave mother and her two sons. Deed and tax records from Georgia also indicate a consistent pattern of owning slaves. The following is a chronology of his known transactions in Leon County from 1832 to 1836:

> January 10, 1832 - Chaires, as executor of Davis Floyd's estate, announces a sale of "Negroes, goods, animals and rent" from his plantation.
>
> April 9, 1833 - Chaires conveys to son Joseph and brother Green Hill, for daughter Mary Ann's benefit: Esther, 15/16 years old; Tenah, about 25 years old; Sally, about 28 years old and her infant of 4 years, Kitty; Martha, about 16 years old. (Note that Sally and Kitty also accompany Mary Ann to New Orleans and later appear on a list of slaves belonging to Mary Ann's son Benjamin Burgess.)
>
> May 28, 1833 - Chaires buys from lawyer Leslie A. Thompson for $2,000.00 portions of four city lots and four slaves: Judy, Harry, Fanny, Charity, plus their future issue and increase.

November 2, 1833 - Chaires lends money to Jeremiah Powell and as collateral obtains 23 slaves: Moses, Orsey, John, Nelson, Jim, Lewis, Thomas, Henry, Amy, Kitty, Indy and her child, Nelly, Nancy, Sally, Charlotte, Anna, Leon, Attaway, Logan, Lucy, Henry, Mary.

December 27, 1833 - daughter Mary Ann takes to New Orleans a Negro woman Sally and child Kitty Ann with permission of her brother Joseph and Uncle Green Hill, as instructed by her father.

April 13, 1835 - Chaires sells to Jesse Willis for $9,000.00: Penny, John, Eliza and her child Fanny, James (?), Hanson, Hilery, Bland, George, Liver (or Liner?) and infant Charles, Bolton, Amos, Relty (?) and her child Margaret, Saul, Margarett and her son Tom, Mary, May, George, Frank, Ben.

June 12, 1835 - Chaires writes his will and bequeaths to his wife Sarah Powell: "negro man Henry, the Carriage Driver."

November 16, 1836 - Chaires buys from George Fauntleroy for $50,000.00 land in T1R1, SE and 57 slaves: Phil, Noah, Morris Gains, Tom, Jack, Achilles, Harry, Ellick, Billy, Moses, Aaron, Godfrey, George the Elder, Aaron the Elder, Chester, Isaac, Ben, Tom Todd, Tom Evans, Harry (or Henry), George the Younger, William, Dasy the Elder, Kitty, Sally, Betsy, Juliet, Lydia, Eliza, Lucinda, Charlotte, Anna, July, Julia, Anny, Denise (?), Green, John, Elijah, Frank, Solomon, Fanny the Elder, Fanny, Eliza, Lavinia,

Patsy, Jane, Mary, Fanny, Aphin (or Ashin), Eliza, Nancy, Letty, Martha, Mary Catherine and 2 infants and future issue and increase.

June 29, 1842 - Public Sale of slaves as part of foreclosure actions on a mortgage held by Benjamin Chaires's estate for Robert Berry: Charles, Shine, Ed #### Mitchell, Edmund Roberts, Moses (?), ####, Joe, Phoebe, Delia, Henry, H####Carter, Fanny, Mary, Ann, Tom, Sam, Charles, Molly, Kate, Lindon, March, ###n, Alexander, Graywood, La#### ##ewton, Cuffe, Castelo, Silla, Dilly ####ia, Ginny, Sarah, Beek, Nancy, Pa### ###, Sally, Ana, Henrietta, P### ###, Priscilla, Jim, Victoria and Adam ####nd issue after 20th April, 1840.

SALE ON WEDNESDAY, JUNE 2Q.

Commissioner's

SALE.

In pursuance of a decree made at April Term, 1842, of the Superior Court of the Middle District of Florida, in and for the County of Leon, sitting in Chancery, made in a certain cause between JOSEPH CHAIRES, Executor of Ben Chaires, deceased, Petitioner for the foreclosure of a Mortgage, and ROBERT H. BERRY, defendant, and by virtue of the execution issued to me to enforce said decree, I shall, on the 29th day of June, 1842, at the Plantation called the FAUNTLEROY PLACE, on the public road leading from Tallahassee to Blocker's Cross Road, in said county of Leon, within legal hours, proceed to sell at public outcry to the highest bidder for cash, the following

SLAVES

Included in said Mortgage, viz :

Charles, Shine, Ed and Mitchell, Edmund Roberts, Moses, Jane, Joe, Phœbe, Delia, Henry, Harriet, Carter, Fanny, Mary, Ann, Tom, Sarah, Charles, Molly, Kate, Lindon, March, John, Alexander, Graywood, Lary, G---- Newton, Cuffe, Castelo, Silla, Dilly ---in, Ginny, Sarah, Beck, Nancy, Patie, ---inah, Sally, Ana, Henrietta, Betsey, ---ah, Priscilla, Jim, Victoria and Adam, and issue after 20th April, 1840.

CHARLES S. SIBLEY,

Commissioner in Chancery, and Elisor in said case,
Appointed by the ---- said Court to make said sale.

Tallahassee, May 27, 1842.

The State Archives of Florida, Florida Memory,
http://floridamemory.com/items/show/34910

82

Planters of Chaires's status were constantly buying and selling huge tracts of land along with the buildings and slaves that went with them, so at any specific time it would be difficult to establish the total number of slaves in his possession. He no doubt owned slaves in other counties where he had vast land holdings as well, but an accounting of those slave properties are reliant on continuing research.

Benjamin Chaires's estate continued to pay taxes on slaves until 1847, and his wife owned slaves at Verdura, as did her estate until the year after her death. The following slave data was taken from Leon County tax records:

Year	Slaves
Benjamin Chaires (d.1838)	
1839 (Est.)	80
1843 (Est.)	88
1844 (Est.)	75
1845 (Est.)	181
1846 (Est.)	182
1847 (Est.)	182
Mrs. Sarah Powell Chaires (d.1846)	
1844	23
1845	50
1846	47
1847	47

Treatment of Slaves

When studying slavery of the antebellum South, the question of slave treatment is always lurking in the back of one's mind. Was Chaires a "kind" master? Or was he one who delegated harsh treatments through his overseers and drivers? An abolitionist, Amos Dresser, who visited Tallahassee in 1835, indicated in two letters he sent from the capital city to a compatriot in the north, that life was extremely bleak for Tallahassee area slaves. Dresser made the interesting observation that, when visiting the South, if one did not physically visit a plantation, and stayed only in the nearby town or city, you would not have thought slaves were treated badly. It was not something openly talked about. One slave owner claimed that he never let his family see or even know about the punishments inflicted on his slaves; he kept the awful truth hidden. He admitted that if his children witnessed such things, it would "harden and brutalize their minds." There is no question that slaves in Leon County were abused, harshly disciplined and humiliated for the smallest offenses.

Dresser's visit to Tallahassee was contemporaneous with another abolitionist's activities in Louisiana: Arthur Tappan. Mr. Tappan was busy there distributing anti-slavery tracts to slaves and to those who sympathized with their plight. Tallahassee's *Floridian and Advocate* included a description of Tappan's activities as well as a narration of the lashing and banishment of Dresser from Nashville, Tennessee for having circulated anti-slavery broadsides in that city. Both of these men were denigrated by slave owners in Middle Florida, so much so that planters gathered for a meeting at Shell Point on September 26, 1835, to counteract the abolitionists' efforts with resolutions of their own defending their right to hold black human beings in bondage. The following resolutions made during that meeting, illustrate the fear, paranoia and anger of the slave holders. They threatened that abolition would have potentially grave consequences for the union, some twenty-six years before the attack on Fort Sumter.

> Resolved, That we, of all parties, as much as we respect and adore the union of these States, do look upon any interference upon the subject of our slave rights, by either the people of the non slave [sic] holding States, or the Congress of the United States, as consequently, directly and unavoidably, involving the existence of this Union.

Resolved, That feeling that sentiment which we believe to be one & undivied [*sic*] in the whole slave portion of this country, we do now *formally* and *solemnly*, protest against any interference by the Congress of the United States upon this subject, either in the Territories or District of Columbia, and that we will vow the agitation of this question in said district as the opening scene to that fearful political drama now in rehearsal.

Slaves worked extremely long and physically demanding hours; if their tasks were not completed, they could expect whippings on bare skin with a cattle skin or wooden paddle. Lashings were often counted in the hundreds. Sometimes slaves would be locked in stocks well into the night. Food was scarce. Some plantation owners provided only corn bread, which had to be eaten quickly, without a rest, in order to get back to work. Meat was provided by some masters, but was not the norm. The complaints of sick slaves were often ignored or punished, so ailing slaves frequently died untreated while working in the fields.

The description of Chaires in his obituary paints a picture of an intelligent and compassionate individual. But were these characteristics extended to the treatment of his slaves? The following excerpt from the letter he wrote to Thomas Fitch in 1820 may provide a clue: "N. B. The violins for the negroes [*sic*] cannot be gotten here they were all Burnt or broken you might get them in St. Marys—please don't fail to do this." Concern also seems evident in the 1820 purchase of slaves he made with Fitch in which there seems to have been an effort to keep slave families together (See listing above). His participation in the Fellenburg Institute would seem to reflect a liberal attitude toward the education of blacks in the community. In addition, the slave Henry Richardson, "Old Henry," whom he had bequeathed to his wife in his will, is said to be buried less than twenty feet from Chaires and his wife in the family cemetery. Indeed, there is a small brick "crypt" located directly behind Sarah's grave. It has no marker and seems too small for a grown man, but could it be the final resting place of a beloved slave? Or... was Chaires hiding his crimes of punishment as did many of his fellows?

Amos Dresser wrote of a conversation he had with slave owner "Col. W." during his Tallahassee visit. Col. W. opined that harsh treatment of his slaves was justifiable if it caused them to work harder and thereby produce a larger crop. This was followed up later in the evening when a "Mr. C." gave Dresser a ride home. When Dresser asked Mr. C. his opinion of justifying harsh treatment for slaves as long as it resulted in a higher yield of crops, Mr. C. said he agreed. When Dresser said he objected to that point of view, Mr. C. said nothing more.

A bit of speculation is called for here: "Col. W." may well have been Colonel George T. Ward, future son-in-law and neighbor of Benjamin Chaires. But, who was "Mr. C."? Maybe it was Ben Chaires, and, if so, it's conceivable that he would have held opinions about slave treatment similar to those of Col. W., but there were many "Mr. C.s" living in Leon County in 1835.

CHAPTER 6
Death, Family, and Beyond

And in the end…

Benjamin Chaires passed away on October 4, 1838, presumably of Yellow Fever. His sudden death was certainly unexpected as he died at age 52, in the prime of his life. In a sense, he was "just getting started." The loss to his friends and cohorts is expressed in his obituary:

> He was the wealthiest planter and capitalist in Florida, and among the most efficient in the South. Florida has sustained a loss in his death which cannot soon be supplied. His enterprise gave an impulse to many of our public improvements, and we know he intended to aid warmly and liberally others in contemplation.

The obituary in full paints a picture of a highly respected, thoughtful, intelligent, and resourceful man. He seems to have been devoted to his family. His opinions were important to others. He certainly was ambitious in acquiring land and business opportunities; obviously he was very interested in making money. Chaires was a man of his time: he would not have supported the abolition of slavery, but he may have cared deeply about some of his slaves on a personal level. He rubbed elbows with the well-connected and the well-known politicians of his day, such as Robert Duval, Andrew Jackson, and Richard Keith Call. He often took chances, sometimes with questionable results. He often played the part of a civil servant. He helped lay out the streets of Louisville, Milledgeville, and Jacksonville. He donated land for the St. Johns County courthouse. He served as president of the Board of Aldermen in St. Augustine and, with empathy for the emigrant Indians, recommended to the President of the United States that the boundaries of their reservation be expanded so they would have access to better land. A family story indicates that he provided safe haven on his land for some Seminoles around the time of removal. He served as a judge, bank president, railroad "czar," and appointed county commissioner.

A seemingly disconnected anecdote may provide another glimpse into Chaires's character: When prominent Leon County citizen and future U. S. Senator, James Westcott, challenged Thomas Baltzell, future member of the Supreme Court, to a duel "over the line" at Brown's Ferry in Alabama in 1834, Leslie A. Thompson, who at the time was a cashier in the Central Bank, agreed to be Westcott's second. Chaires got wind of the situation and sent a note to Thompson saying that if he participated in any way in the duel, he would lose his job. Perhaps Chaires disapproved of dueling. Perhaps he was concerned about the reputation of the bank with one of its employees participating in such an activity. Or, maybe he just didn't want Thompson, an old friend and cohort, to be involved in an illegal act.

Chaires was tenacious, never admitting fault or giving in to defeat: this may have been his most distinguishing trait. When accused of trespassing, he fought the charges to the bitter end. He gave up a position in history by declining his nomination to the Florida Constitutional Convention: for him, business, and his commitment to it, was more important. He was something of a visionary, full of energy and ambition, but sometimes his impetuous nature led to lapses in judgment. He helped provide rations for the Indians, but became embroiled in a scandalous effort to bribe a fellow bidder. He trespassed, not once but twice, onto land he did not own and damaged the acreage while also making "improvements" not sought after by the owners.

Ben Chaires was, seemingly, a stereotype of an elite plantation owner. It is easy to imagine him sitting on the veranda of his palatial home drinking mint julips, surveying his cotton fields, and guiding his slaves in their tasks. He was also much like his fellow Nucleus members: wealthy, ambitious, rather greedy, and he found enjoyment in "playing the game." But, he was more than that. He was totally immersed in the political landscape of his time, and, because his interests were varied, his associates varied. This led him to affiliations beyond just members of The Nucleus, as he also joined with members of The Saints in the town of St. Joseph. He was not content to grow cotton and tend to his farms. He didn't just participate in civic and business opportunities, he led the way. He was not a prince of the Cotton Kingdom, but a flawed king. He was a man who looked to the future, but, like many of his compatriots, he became entangled in the webs of Florida's economic and political landscape that eventually led to a devastating financial collapse for the new territory. Chaires saw the need for the development of nearby ports and harbors so farmers and planters could export their produce to foreign markets, and he knew that the collaboration of government, banks and railroads would further this along. He certainly recognized the benefits of using modern technology, such as steam driven ships and locomotives, but the watery environments of Middle Florida foiled his attempts to tame the swamps time and time again. Ultimately, and ironically, it may have been a tiny, unseen inhabitant of those bug-filled marshes that brought him down before his work was done.

The Family

Benjamin Chaires and Sarah Powell had ten children: Joseph (1811-1866), Mary Ann (1813-1845), Green D. (1816-1885), Benjamin Jr. (1821-1873) born in Georgia; and Furman (1823-1867), Sara Jane (1825-1859), Martha (1827-1866), Thomas Butler (1828-1880), Charles Powell (1830-1881), and Josephine (1832-1840), born in Florida. All but Josephine lived to adulthood. Green D. was the longest lived of Benjamin's children and the last to die, succumbing to a possible urinary infection at the age of 69 in March of 1885. Benjamin Chaires was to have thirty-five grandchildren, but knew only two: William Gaither Burgess, Jr., and Benjamin C. Burgess, sons of his estranged daughter Mary Ann. Of Chaires's immediate family, his wife Sarah and children Joseph, Green D., Thomas Butler, Charles Powell, Mary Ann, Josephine, and grandchildren Benjamin C. Burgess, William G. Burgess, Jr., and Maria Chaires (Furman's daughter) are thought to be buried with him in the cemetery at Verdura, although not all of those have grave markers. Timelines, obituaries and epitaphs (if available) for each of Chaires's children, and some grandchildren can be found in the Appendix. Because the vagaries of his life caused the Chaires family to lose the Verdura property, a full chapter on youngest son Charles Powell Chaires will follow.

Benjamin Chaires's Estate

Oldest son Joseph became executor of his father's estate, and on October 13, he published a notice in the *Floridian and Advocate* stating that anyone having a claim against the estate should notify him "within the time prescribed by law." In his will, Benjamin Chaires intended for his wife and nine of his children to each have a tenth of his land holdings. That would have meant that each child (with the exception of Mary Ann, to whom he bequeathed only $10,000) would inherit ±890 acres in Leon County. After the death of the youngest daughter Josephine in 1840, that figure would have increased to ±988 acres and, after Sarah Powell's death in 1846, each heir could have expected a one- eighth interest in the 500 cleared acres of Verdura that had been left to Sarah Powell. (In addition to land, he left his wife his furniture and household goods, plus one-tenth of his personal estate for the rest of her life.) The tax records, census records, and probate files for the children of Benjamin Chaires do reflect that property ownership in the area of 1,000 acres was the norm. Of course, individuals purchased, inherited or obtained through marriage, properties in addition to those acquired from their father.

At the time of his death, Chaires's estate included almost 10,000 acres of land in Leon County. These holdings were additional to thousands of acres he had purchased or claimed in St. Johns, Volusia, Jackson, Jefferson, Gadsden, Hamilton, Alachua, and Nassau counties. When he died, his land holdings in Township 1, Range 2 South and East, the location of Verdura Plantation, were comprised of 4,640 acres, which he had purchased between the years 1826 and 1837. In 1858, some of this property, the Verdura mansion and about 720 acres around it, found its way into the possession of Chaires's two youngest sons, Thomas Butler and Charles Powell, when their siblings relinquished their inherited shares. Charles Powell also acquired some of his father's lands situated in portions of Sections 1, 2 and 3 of T1R1, SE. This plantation eventually became Charles Powell's home and was known as "Ever May" or the "May Place." Deed records show that Thomas Butler's portion of his father's estate, located in T1R1, SE and T1R2, SE, was later referred to as "Tiger Tail," possibly named for the Seminole Chief with whom he was said to be friendly. Thomas Butler shared ownership of Verdura with Charles Powell from 1858 to 1877: from the beginning of the secession crisis, through the Civil War and Reconstruction.

Various tax and deed records show that sons Joseph and Furman owned land immediately east of Verdura, and that Southwood Plantation, to the west, was owned by George T. Ward, husband of Chaires's daughter Sarah Jane. The 1,000 acres Sarah received from her father's estate was joined with Ward's property to form the totality of Southwood Plantation. Sarah Jane's grave is located behind Southwood's main house. Chaires's daughter Martha was the mistress of Bolton Plantation, on the northern shores of Lake Lafayette, prior to her marriage to Robert H. Gamble. Bolton was the name of a college in Baltimore, Maryland, that Martha had attended. Sons Green D. and Furman acquired land in the Forbes Purchase, southwest of Verdura, and Green D. also owned land between today's Centerville and Miccosukee Roads.

Benjamin Chaires owned another plantation east of Southwood that he had purchased from George Fauntleroy. This

1,200 acre property was split almost in half by the St. Augustine Road. Chaires paid only one-half of the $50,000 price tag on the plantation so, in 1842, the estate held an auction with some 32 slaves put up for bids in order to pay off the $25,000 balance. This property, which retained the name "Fauntleroy," became the home of his son Benjamin Junior, and later, of his grandson, Benjamin Cadwallader Chaires ("Ben C."). At the same time Benjamin purchased Fauntleroy, he bought a larger plantation of 2,000 acres, known as Cornucopia, an "auxiliary" plantation belonging to John Parkhill (Green D.'s father-in-law), located 2 miles east of Bel-Air, south of Tallahassee in the piney flatlands. Bel-Air was a nineteenth century country retreat to which Tallahasseans would escape the summer heat and swamp gas from nearby marshes. Cornucopia was also later owned by Benjamin Junior. (Another Benjamin Chaires, known as Benjamin, Sr., was the son of Green Hill Chaires. Benjamin, Sr. is often confused with the Ben Chaires of this narrative, which has caused misinformation in family and public records.)

Farther to the east and northeast of Verdura were the plantations of Benjamin's brothers Green Hill and Thomas Peter. Green's plantation, Evergreen Hill, was on the northern shore of Lake Lafayette. It was Green Hill's family that was the target of a horrific Indian massacre in July of 1839, in which his wife was shot and two children were burned alive when the Indians set the house afire. The victims' remains were buried in a small family cemetery located on Old Dirt Road in Tallahassee. Tom Peter's plantation, Woodlawn, was within the present community of Chaires. The graves of Tom and his wife Angelina are located in the yard of a private property owner.

There were no documents found in the public records that officially conveyed any of Benjamin Chaires's property to his heirs. Evidently these transactions were conducted privately among family members. This premise is supported in a petition to the court filed on June 25, 1873, by the heirs requesting that John A. Henderson become administrator of Benjamin Chaires's Estate (the original executors, Green H. Chaires and Joseph

Chaires had died). It states in this petition that Joseph Chaires, while administrator, "divided much of the realty of the estate." Henderson became administrator on July 3rd and on August 25, 1873, a claim was filed against the estate by the "General Government" for $1,000.00 on a grant of 17,500 acres; these were the "Alachua Lands." The heirs then wanted Henderson to be allowed to "make distribution of the undivided lands [the lands in various counties of Florida] and to collect the said claim."

CHAPTER 7
Verdura

Verdura Plantation, or The Verdura Place, in its early years, was quintessentially representative of the elite planter culture. The mansion home, constructed in the Greek revival style, was vast in size and opulent in its decor. It was a place that signaled to all comers that the owner was a very rich and important person. Sadly, Chaires may have only lived at Verdura for a few months prior to his death in 1838. The ruins of Benjamin Chaires's plantation house, southeast of Tallahassee, have come to symbolize the excess that was the Cotton Kingdom and the original sin of slavery that eventually destroyed it. Chaires named his opulent plantation Verdura, in honor of the abundant greenery of the area. The mansion house sat on the edge of the Cody Escarpment southeast of Tallahassee about 12 miles. The elevation is about 125 feet above sea level. The land below the escarpment, known as the Coastal Plain, is sandy and flat, and the vegetation is primarily scrub pine and scrub oak, with intermittent lakes and ponds. It is a remnant of the ancient gulf water front where the waves wore down the edge of the Tallahassee Hills. Above, on the scarp, the vegetation is thick with live oaks, Yaupon holly, and other native trees and vines. In more recent years, the farm lands that were once white with cotton became part of the great timber industry begun by the St. Joe Paper Company in the 1940s. Remnants of their planted slash pines can be seen today. It is now, as it was when the property was purchased by Chaires (1827 to 1837), "out in the middle of nowhere" and is still in private ownership. No one knows whether Chaires considered all 4,560 acres of land he owned in that area to be part of Verdura or if the 500 acres around the Big House that he left to his wife was his vision of the plantation's boundaries. Later, when Charles Powell and Thomas Butler owned the property it constituted 680 acres, which increased to 1,000 with contiguous lands purchased by

Charles. The house was large: 50 feet deep by 80 across. Five columns graced the east and west elevations, which supported verandas on both sides. The house had a "slave basement," a grand staircase in the center of the house, a marble floor on the first level, and an attic with a view to the south, to the Gulf coast.

The view toward the gulf coast from "Butler Hill" at Verdura.

Verdura was typical of an elite antebellum plantation. In addition to the Big House, there was a detached kitchen, barns, livery stable, a root cellar, blacksmith shop, slave quarters, a slave cemetery, clay pits, wells, and privies, as well as cisterns, a cotton gin, and a family graveyard. Water was also available from a creek down the hill to the east of the house. Today, all that remains of the mansion are the 10 columns and a huge mound of bricks where the walls of the house fell after a fire in the 1880s. The oven in the kitchen is still visible, as are the remains of a storage building just north of the kitchen. There are large patches of paved brick in the front and back of the house ruins, which probably indicate walkways and entrances to the house and basement. As was the custom of the day, the house was probably whitewashed and may have had green trim and shutters. The slave-made brick columns had been covered with stucco, probably whitewashed, which is breaking away due to time, weather and vandalism.

The mansion ruins at Verdura looking east.

Historic Descriptions of the Mansion

In February of 1839, Daniel Wiggins, a sojourner from New York looking to make his fortune in Florida, traveled to Tallahassee from Richmond, a small settlement on the St. Marks River. On the way, he wrote,

> A little before I got to the Augustine road [*sic*] I passed by a large and elegant house that belongs

97

to Mr. Ben [S]hears heirs very rich people. It is
the best dwelling house I have seen in Florida—
the body of the house [is] brick and each side
and the whole length of the house is a porch or
piazza supported by long brick columns.

In 1858, Charles Powell and Thomas Butler Chaires placed
an advertisement to sell Verdura in the Tallahassee *Floridian
and Journal* of October 2nd; the house is described as follows:

Upon the premises is a GOOD BRICK
DWELLING, three stories high, and containing
thirteen large rooms. The outhouses are of Brick
and built in the most substantial manner.

A 1947 article in the Tallahassee *Democrat* describes the
roof of the mansion as having had a center portion of gray slate
with the sides of wooden shingles. (It should be noted that a
surface collection of artifacts conducted around the mansion
ruins in 2000 resulted in zero pieces of slate collected.) The
article also mentions green window shutters. Susan Eppes
describes the Pine Hill mansion, a plantation contemporary with
Verdura, which was owned by one of the Bradford brothers and
was located north of the present I-10 / Thomasville Road
interchange, as follows:

In the grove of towering pines stood a large and
stately mansion; white and green, as a country
house should be. Rose-gardens and shrubbery of
many kinds, grew around the house, while away,
on every side, spread smooth and velvety lawns.

Eppes also tells us that the Pine Hill great house was three
stories, had high ceilings, large windows, wide doors, sat on the
crest of a hill, and had a circular driveway. Although the Pine
Hill big house was of frame construction, and the Verdura

mansion was masonry, the Pine Hill attributes, similar to those in descriptions of Verdura, serve to substantiate those descriptions.

Benjamin Chaires's great-granddaughter Alice Burroughs Chaires, who had visited Verdura as a child, described the house and property in an interview for the Tallahassee *Democrat* in 1963. According to her description, the house was located on the top of a hill circled by a stream at its base. The house faced south and a view of the Gulf could be seen from the attic. There were five columns covered with curved brick on the east and west sides of the house. The rooms had high ceilings, and each room had a fireplace. There was an aboveground basement and two upper stories with a double stairway that swept up from the first to the second story. There were drawing rooms on either side of a foyer with doors that could be opened to form a ballroom eighty feet long; the floor was of marble. There was a massive Dutch oven in the side yard. Miss Chaires describes the approach to the house: "The front drive which curved up the hill, branched off to lead under the portico from where a stairway led to the front hall on the second floor."

In September of 1999, Henry Agnew "Hank" Chaires, a great-great-great grandson of Benjamin Chaires, was interviewed by this author. In that interview, Chaires described a 1934 horseback trip to Verdura with his grandfather, Bradford Chaires, son of Samuel Parkhill Chaires. At the time of their visit, portions of the walls of the house were still standing and remnants of a wooden floor could be seen inside the structural remains. Bradford Chaires had described the house to his grandson as having had a sitting room, large dining room, smoking and game room, and a closet on the first floor, with a central staircase leading to the second floor. He also told him that there was a master bedroom on the second floor with three adjoining rooms, and five small bedrooms on the third floor where he, Bradford, had slept as a boy.

Chaires recalled that his grandfather described "bathrooms" on each floor of the house with tubs for bathing. There were no privies for family members because they used chamber pots or

99

slop buckets inside the house, which were then taken by slaves (and later by servants) to a wagon fitted with a tank. When the tank was full of waste, the wagon was driven to the creek at the bottom of the hill and the tank emptied.

Archaeology at Verdura

The remains of the detached kitchen and the possible food storage building (previously referred to as the North Structure) beside it have been investigated archaeologically. It was found that the storage building had a masonry floor, two rooms and sufficient footers to support a two story building. It was constructed of brick and may have had a root cellar or spring house associated with it. Prior to the excavation, the remains were thought to have been a slave quarter, but the structural remains and artifacts do not indicate that the building was any kind of domicile.

The detached kitchen was tested archaeologically and found to have had a clay floor rather than masonry. It was larger than the storage building, and the remains of its oven (referred to as a Dutch oven) are extant. Artifacts taken from a test pit were consistent with a food preparation facility. It is thought that some of the paved brick at the rear of the mansion is part of a walkway that led from the kitchen to the slave basement beneath the house.

The masonry floor of the food storage building with the
remains of the Dutch oven visible in the background
to the right. Photo taken by Fred Gaske.

In 2000, Daniel Fletcher, a descendent of the Chaires family, was visiting the cemetery and noticed that plowing around the house ruins had brought numerous artifacts to the surface. With the help of Florida State University archaeology faculty, St. Joe agreed to allow a group of students and professionals to collect artifacts and to map the site. The artifacts consisted of construction materials such as window glass, nails, bricks and brick fragments, limestone, many types of ceramics, copious amounts of oyster shell, mortar fragments, bottle glass, metals (most unidentifiable), as well as faunal and plant materials. The analysis of this artifact collection is included in this author's research thesis. The artifacts were returned to the St. Joe Company at the conclusion of the artifact analysis.

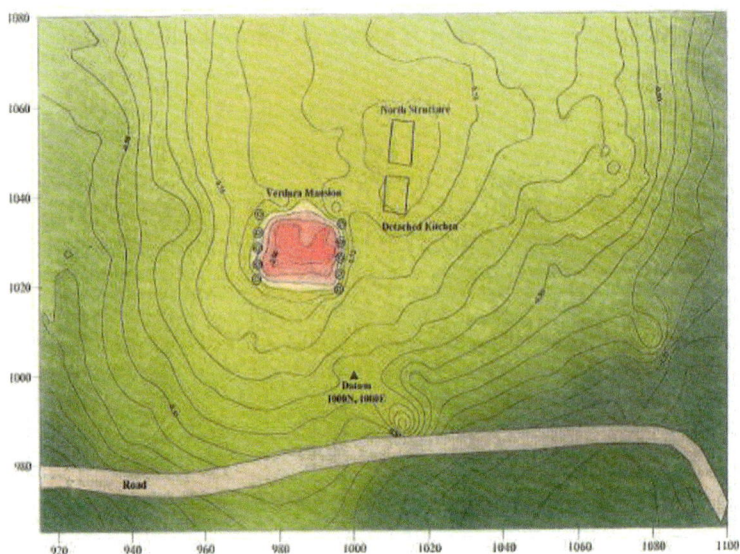

Site map of Verdura generated during the 2000 surface collection.

A Mysterious Rendering

An original pencil drawing of the Verdura mansion has been in the possession of Anne Mintz, a great-great-great-great granddaughter of Benjamin Chaires via his daughter Sarah Jane, who was married to George T. Ward of Southwood Plantation. Reproductions of this drawing frequently accompany newspaper articles and local histories about Verdura. Mintz's family has believed the drawing to be the work of her great-grandfather, James Grant, who was a Confederate soldier and whose sketches of his war time experiences are also in Mintz's collection, and the style of the drawings bear a strong resemblance to the Verdura picture. The family estimates that the rendering of Verdura was executed between 1864 and 1867 and maintains that it has "always been among the family papers."

102

Mintz pencil drawing of the Verdura mansion.

The rendering of the mansion seems to have a conflicting history, however. In a collection of family materials provided by Chaires descendent Daniel Fletcher, there is a note written from one Edwin Pugsley to a Mr. Conrad dated April 5, 1961, in which he says,

> It occurred to me that you might not have a sketch of the original house at Verdura. Mr. Patterson's mother a girl of 17 [the sister of Bradford Chaires] was living in the house when it burned in 1885.... In 1931 an architect measured the site and columns and from Mrs. Patterson's description drew up a sketch about 15" X 20" which original Mr. Patterson has.

A 1947 article in the Tallahassee *Democrat* stated, "From the columns and photos of wall sections before they fell, and description by persons who lived in Verdura, Gene Fitchner,

103

architect, made a pen and ink drawing of the mansion for posterity."

The Mintz drawing is most assuredly rendered in pencil, not pen and ink, and includes the word Verdura drawn in thick lettering at the lower right of the picture; the frequently used copy accompanying Verdura histories does not, but in all other details it appears to be the same. To add to the confusion, the drawing appears in Clifton Paisley's *The Red Hills of Florida, 1528-1865* and does not include the word Verdura at the bottom, but farther down Fitchner's signature can be seen.

According to descendent Hank Chaires, his grandfather Bradford (grandson of Green D.), was raised in the community of Chaires and did not ever live at Verdura, yet his sister said she did. Attached to Pugsley's note is a copy of the drawing which appears to be identical to the one in Mintz's collection with the exception of the word Verdura at the bottom. (It is certainly possible that the bottom of the drawing might not have been included in copies of the drawing.) Hank Chaires owned a copy which his mother "bought" from Patterson in the 1970s.

The Fire

Family history maintains that the Verdura mansion burned in 1885, but nothing was found in the public documents or in contemporary newspapers to confirm that date. In December of 1882, three articles appeared in local papers reporting that the mansion house of Charles R. Chaires, only son of Joseph, had burned. It was described as "the old family mansion and was prized on that account." Were the reporters confused as to which "Charles" owned the burned mansion? Was Joseph's mansion considered an old family mansion? Did both homes burn in the 1880s? Regardless of the date, the magnificent house was gone. Parts of walls remained standing for several years, but eventually the rubble heap of fallen bricks grew to a depth of around six feet. Because most of the remaining bricks are "brickbats," it is thought that many full-sized bricks were salvaged, probably along with other re-usable architectural materials.

There are different theories as to the cause of the fire. The most common of them is that it was caused by workmen raking and burning leaves. One version states that a tree near the house caught fire, sparks landed on the wooden roof shingles, and the fire spread. Pugsley relates that "some of the help were burning trash in the front yard when a tree caught and set the porch roofs on fire." Bradford Chaires remembered hearing that lightning during a severe thunder storm had started the fire. Another family descendent is suspicious that the fire was set intentionally by family members eager to be released from the responsibilities of caring for the "white elephant."

There seems to have been a period of intense building on both of Charles Powell's plantations between 1883 and 1889. Chancery Court records show that his estate purchased a considerable amount of nails, boards and lumber, hinges, screws, locks, and barrels of lime for a house at Verdura and for a house at Ever May. The location of the house (or houses) at Verdura is unknown, and it is not known whether it was a small house built for a tenant farmer or whether it was a larger dwelling to be used by a member of the family—perhaps as new accommodations replacing those of the burned mansion. The estate also paid for repairs to houses at Ever May and Verdura, as well as for the repair and construction of chimneys and a cotton gin.

The Family Graveyard

The graveyard at Verdura is about 300 yards to the east of the mansion ruins. It is surrounded by a thick brick wall with an opening on the west side, facing the mansion. It has long been subjected to the overgrowth of vegetation, vandalism, weather, general decay, and falling trees and limbs. The first burial there was that of Benjamin Chaires, who died on October 4, 1838. More than 175 years after his death, visitors permitted on the almost mythical plantation site can still read the inscription engraved on his very prominent tombstone. Chaires's burial was followed by that of grandson William Gaither Burgess, Jr., who died two days later. Other family members buried there with visible grave markers include youngest daughter Josephine, who died at age 8 in 1840, Russell Ormand (wife of Joseph) and her sister Helen Ormand, who died within 2 days of each other during the Yellow Fever epidemic that struck Tallahassee in 1841. Oldest daughter Mary Anne Chaires Burgess was buried there in 1845, followed the next year by her mother Sarah Powell Chaires in 1846. Another grandchild, Maria, daughter of Furman Chaires, was buried there at the age of nine months, eleven days, in the mid-1840s. Grandson Benjamin Burgess died after a protracted illness in 1860 and is buried close to his mother and brother. Green D. Chaires was buried at Verdura in 1885 next to his first wife Ann Maria Parkhill Chaires who died in 1861.

A survey of rural cemeteries conducted in 1973 by the Colonial Dames XVII Century listed twenty graves in the cemetery. Only 12 of those have markers. It is unknown if there had ever been markers for the unmarked graves, if the deceased had been buried without markers, or if those 12 souls were actually buried at Verdura. All of these unmarked graves are also included in a more extensive list of burial places for many Chaires family members found in a family Bible record kept by Thomas Butler and his wife Sarah Salter, and later reproduced by Virginia Chaires Webb in 1964. Those listed as being buried at Verdura but without grave markers include: sons Thomas Butler Chaires in 1880 and Charles Powell in 1881; Charles's first wife Sarah Ann Raines whose death date is unknown; and Thomas's wife Sarah Salter in 1892, which would have been the final burial in the graveyard. Also said to be buried at Verdura without grave markers are: Green D.'s son Joseph George in 1863; his grandson Samuel Parkhill Chaires II, also in 1863; his son-in-law Jasper Scruggs; and his granddaughter-in-law Willie Lipford Farmer with her unnamed daughter, whose burial dates are unknown.

When Benjamin Chaires wrote his will, he left to his wife their favorite slave, Henry the Carriage Driver. Henry is thought to have been buried within 20 feet of Chaires and his wife in the family cemetery. During a volunteer clean-up project by members of the Panhandle Archaeological Society at Tallahassee (PAST) in 2007, a small brick crypt was found to the east and just behind the grave site of Sarah Powell Chaires. It is quite small, seemingly too small to hold a human adult. Perhaps Henry Richardson was of small stature and became even smaller in old age.

The Chaires family graveyard at Verdura after a clean-up in 2007. (Joseph's grave is the obelisk in the foreground; Benjamin's grave is topped by an urn with Sarah's grave just to the left).

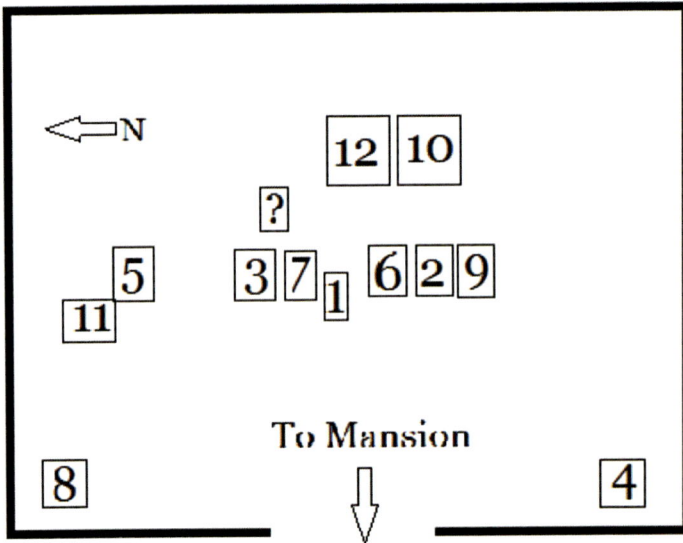

Layout of Chaires family graves at Verdura (not to scale).

1. Benjamin Chaires, 1838
2. William Gaither Burgess, 1838
3. Josephine Chaires, 1840
4. Helen Ormand, 1841
5. Russell Ormand, 1841
6. Mary Anne Chaires Burgess, 1845
7. Sarah Powell Chaires, 1846
8. Maria Chaires, c.1847
9. Benjamin Chaires Burgess, 1860
10. Ann Parkhill Chaires, 1861
11. Joseph Chaires, 1866
12. Green D. Chaires, 1885
?   Brick Crypt

The number of individuals housed in slave dwellings varied according to the wealth and concern of the plantation owner. Studies have shown that occupation rates were highly variable. John W. Blassingame reports variations in number from as few as 3.7 slaves per house to as many as ten to twelve individuals per cabin in general. Ulrich Phillips and James Glunt report that there were 155 slaves at El Destino Plantation in Jefferson County, Florida, and they were housed in 20 slave cabins, an average of 7.75 slaves per dwelling. Glen Doran and Rochelle Marrinan note that in Leon County in 1860, there were 69 slaves on the Bannerman Place, at an occupancy rate of 4 to 5 people per house. They also report that the Theus-Roberts Farm, also in Leon County, provided shelter for 4 to 5 individuals per dwelling.

Prior to 1850, while Benjamin and Sarah Chaires were living, and for the duration of their estates, records show that the slave count at Verdura went from a low of 80 to a high of 302. The average number of slaves for nine years of available data is 174.6. Using the aforementioned Leon County figures as a guide (a low of 4 and a high of 7.75 per dwelling), one could estimate that between 23 and 44 slave houses would have been necessary to accommodate the Benjamin Chaires family bondsmen.

Due to the large landholdings that Chaires owned (and it is not evident from the public records just where he perceived the parameters of Verdura to have been), it could be deduced that not all of his slaves were housed at Verdura. William Warren Rogers states, in reference to Goodwood's owner Bryan Croom, that "Bryan's property had become so large that he split it into two farming operations and, in effect, into two plantations, each with its own overseers and slaves." It is well within the range of probability that some portions of Chaires's landholdings were perceived by him to have been separate plantations and that his slaves would have been housed at different locations. For example, in 1836, Chaires bought the plantation known as Fauntleroy along with 57 slaves. This land was located on both sides of the St. Augustine Road and included parcels in Sections 10 and 11 in Township 1 South, Range 1 East, about three miles from Verdura. The 1840 census lists only one domicile for the Benjamin Chaires family, under oldest son Joseph as head of household. It may have been that since blacks were not counted on the census as "real people," they were all listed under one domicile because they "belonged" to Chaires, even if they may have actually lived on plantations other than Verdura.

The 1850 census reveals that Charles Powell and Thomas Butler shared a domicile, presumably Verdura, and the 1850 tax records show that they jointly owned 118 slaves. Using the same figures stated above, between approximately 15 and 30 cabins would have been necessary to house their slaves. The 1860 census shows Charles Powell with 28 slave houses and Thomas Butler with 20, providing shelter for a combined total of 165 slaves or 3.43 slaves per domicile. Again, these figures may pertain only to Verdura or, more likely, they may apply to the combined plantations of the two brothers: Verdura, Ever May and Tiger Tail.

Construction and Layout of Slave Quarters at Verdura

There is very little physical evidence as to the location or construction of the slave quarters at Verdura. No documentary information was discovered that described the layout of the quarters. Hank Chaires remembers being told by his grandfather in the 1930s that the slave quarters were located to the northwest of the mansion, "within sight of the house." Hank Chaires's recollection was reinforced by a statement made by the employee of St. Joe Company, who was responsible for the clearing of the site in November of 1999. He stated that he had been told of the presence of a slave cemetery "down by the creek" to the northwest of the house. A walk-over of that part of the Verdura site did not reveal any remains that could have been interpreted as dwellings or a cemetery.

In the 1858 advertisement to sell Verdura (see page 98), one of the selling points was that, "The outhouses are of Brick and built in the most substantial manner." It is hard to say if the brothers might have been referring to the slave quarters, but knowing from historical accounts that Benjamin Chaires had a liking for brick manufacturing, and if other "outhouses" on the property were of brick, it is probable that slave housing was made of brick.

Hank Chaires was told that there had been a slave quarter directly behind the mansion. He may have had in mind the remains of a building previously referred to as a storage building (or North Structure) related to the nearby detached kitchen. This building had a brick foundation, a masonry floor, and brick walls. During the 2000 Surface Survey at Verdura, the west wall and a possible interior wall were uncovered and artifacts collected. Cut nails, window glass fragments, green bottle glass fragments, and a sherd of salt-glazed stoneware were recovered. The follow-up excavation of the building was conducted in 2010. Similar, if not identical, artifacts were recovered at that time.

As for the location of Verdura's slave houses, the closest analogy found to date is an undated sketch map of Woodlawn Plantation, the home of Chaires's younger brother Tom Peter, which indicates that there were sixteen slave houses behind the big house somewhat hidden behind rows of fruit trees. Additionally, a 1967 photograph of the slave house located behind The Columns, prior to its move, may also provide a hint as to the architecture of the slave houses at Verdura.

111

Slave house at The Columns.
Photo courtesy of Richard Parks
and the Florida State Archives,
Florida Memory
http://floridamemory.com/items/
show/46782

While Benjamin Chaires repeatedly bought and sold slaves throughout his lifetime, there are no public records showing transactions involving slaves for either of his two youngest sons, Charles Powell and Thomas Butler, owners of Verdura. They owned slaves, but evidently they either traded them without benefit of legal action or simply allowed nature to take its course with attrition and growth in slave holdings attributable to deaths and births.

When Charles Powell and Thomas Butler shared a domicile, presumably Verdura, the 1850 Slave Schedule shows that together they owned 126 slaves, and as individuals, Charles Powell declared 10 slaves to be his own and Thomas Butler declared eight. Their joint tax records for that year show that they claimed 118 slaves. After 1850, the brothers did not pay joint taxes on slaves. From 1851 to 1855, Charles paid taxes on 65 to 70 slaves; Thomas Butler paid taxes on 60, until 1855 when his slave holdings increased by one. This suggests that the brothers may have split the value of the slaves they had shared at Verdura and used them on their individual plantations as well as on Verdura.

From 1859 to 1863 (the last available tax records during the Civil War), Charles paid taxes on human property that varied in number from 46 to 84 individuals, and Thomas Butler's holdings varied from 45 to 67. The number of slaves for Charles and Thomas on the 1860 census is in excess of that reflected in their taxes. Information supplied for Charles by William Jackson on the census for that year indicates that Charles owned 93 slaves and his brother Thomas owned 72. In 1860, Charles paid taxes on 65 slaves and Thomas paid on 50. During these years, the brothers shared ownership of Verdura and each had his own plantation as well, so it might be inferred that these slaves were being moved from plantation to plantation as needed. Regardless of the numbers, there would have been slave quarters at Verdura after Benjamin Chaires died and his sons took over the planting/farming operations. Their specific locations remain unknown.

Post-war Share Croppers, Servants, and Tenant Farmers

After the War Between the States, sharecropping was instituted county to county across the south. There is no direct evidence of the manner in which it was organized at Verdura, but in 1868, another Chaires family member, Green A. Chaires, a cousin of Charles and Thomas, had his tenant farmers sign employment contracts that spelled out his expectations for his employees. These contracts are listed as "leases" in the Grantors Index in the Leon County Deed Records, but they have more to do with restrictions and obedience than they do rental arrangements. This type of employment, one of many attempted by plantation owners to maintain control over their former slaves, was called a wage-contract system. According to Charles Orser, "Although many kinds of contracts were written immediately after the war, all of them were written to insure that plantation owners received the most labor for their money." These were the only contracts found for Chaires family plantations, so it would seem that other Chaires plantation owners did not go to the same extreme in the hiring of the freedmen. Perhaps Green A. Chaires, having been a successful planter before and after the war, may have needed more employees than others in his family, and therefore wished to have greater control over his hands. The requirements for their employees, however, may have been similar. While wordy, it is interesting to see the detail with which these contracts were written, ironically, for mostly illiterate workers. The Green A. Chaires contracts stipulated that the employees

> shall faithfully industriously and honestly serve their said Employer on any plantation or farm everywhere readily obeying all the commands or directions and each rule and regulation as to the kind of work or mode and manner of doing work: the hours for work for meals for rest and all other matters pertaining to the duties to be performed by them as their said Employer or his agent may command direct or prescribe. Said Employees shall also protect and preserve the property of said Employer and shall not injure, waste or destroy the same and shall not absent themselves from the plantation or farm or quit their work without the consent of said Employer or his Agent and said Employees shall at all times and in all things, behave as good Honest peaceable and industrious servants ought to do in a well regulated and thorough business plantation or farm.
>
> Said Employer agrees to receive said Employees into his service upon the conditions above mentioned. And in consideration of Services and as full compensation for work and labor to be done, rendered and performed as aforesaid Said Employer agrees and binds himself that he will allow and pay said Employees as follows *viz*:

All the cotton corn and half the other products to be grown and gathered on said plantation by said employees by said [*sic*] Except Ten Bales of Cotton of best quality weighing five hundred pounds each and except so much of said Cotton or other products as may be necessary to fully indemnify and make good said Employer for the loss of stock farming implements and for all supplies or goods of any character or indebtedness incurred contingent or otherwise by said employees or any or either of them, and it is expressly understood and agreed upon between the parties to this agreement that said Employer is to have a first preferred and first lien upon and the control and right to dispose of all the crops grown and gathered on said plantation until he shall be fully paid for all claims and indemnified for all losses under the agreement.

As to support and maintenance and necessary supplies of said Employees, during their term of service it is agreed upon between the parties to the Contract as follows viz: that said Employees are to feed clothe and feed [*sic*] themselves and that said Employer is to be in no wise chargeable for any expense on their account and that for a violation of this agreement as aforesaid by said Employees or either of them said Employer or his agent is to have the right to turn from off said plantation and dismiss from his service any Employee so violating this agreement.

No information was found regarding servants or tenant farmers at Verdura until 1873 when the first documentary evidence of tenant farmers as taxpayers is revealed in the Leon

County Tax Records. African-Americans were listed on the tax rolls, but were literally segregated on paper from their white counterparts. In most cases these black taxpayers were sharecroppers or tenant farmers (not land owners), so the records indicate either the employer of the black worker or the name of the plantation where he (or infrequently she) was employed. If the African-American tax-payer did own land, it was often designated as being "near" a particular white person's property. From 1873 to 1881, the number of Charles's and Thomas's tenant farmers varied as they were probably used on their individual plantations in addition to Verdura. The same tenant family names are frequently repeated at various Chaires family plantations.

Tenant Structures

According to Orser, most former slaves did not decide to desert their plantations when freedom came:

> Many preferred to stay in their antebellum plantation homes to see what was going to happen in the South. This decision to stay was based on a complex set of interrelated factors including personal circumstances, the generally poor or non-existent education of plantation blacks, the passing of strict vagrancy laws meant to keep blacks on plantations and a widespread lack of training for anything but plantation agriculture.

It is likely that, at first, slaves who remained on the plantations continued to live in the slave quarters. Most lived in the same houses they had occupied as slaves, and wore clothes and ate food dispensed by the planters, and labored in gangs under the vigilance of bosses, much like those of the antebellum years. As their homes began to deteriorate or become abandoned,

116

new quarters for the tenant farmers were constructed. When planters turned to sharecropping or renting land in the 1870s (as opposed to the wage-contract system), landlords supplied a patch of land and a house to the worker in return for rent, which was often paid as a portion of the harvested crops. A visitor to Leon County in 1885 found that the "huts scattered irregularly over the land" differed markedly from the "regularly laid out quarters" of the slaves he had witnessed forty years earlier. The visitor went on to say, "The rudely built log cabin, with its chimney of sticks and mud, surmounted by four balls of clay, is a type unlike the work of any other home builders with which I am familiar."

It is possible that dozens of tenant structures may have existed on a single plantation. While no occupancy rates were found for tenant housing in Leon County, it might be assumed that each dwelling represented the domicile of a single family of various sizes. There were no data recovered on the number of tenant farmers or sharecroppers present at Verdura until 1873, when black taxpayers were first listed separately in the tax records. Between the years 1873 and 1889, Charles Powell (or his estate) and Thomas Butler (until 1878) had a total of 109 hands with an average of 9 per year for which there are only 12 years of available data. Not all of these would have been housed at Verdura, and they probably worked at all three of the brothers' plantations.

If the parameters of the cultivated fields at Verdura could be determined, it might be possible to narrow the search for remains of tenant structures there. Share renters were often dispersed across the plantation for economic reasons; it was simply more efficient to place tenant structures close to the fields the hands worked. It is highly probable that tenant structures were present in some quantity at Verdura, but with changes in ownership of the property beginning in 1896, until the purchase of the property by the St. Joe Company in 1948, the fate of the tenant houses was in the hands of the property owners. Even if they had survived into the 1940s, it is likely that many unoccupied structural remains were razed with the onset of tree farming by St. Joe.

117

The "Eliteness" of Verdura

Prior to Benjamin Chaires's death and for about eight years thereafter, Verdura would have been considered an elite or upper class plantation. The historical record indicates that Chaires was considered wealthy, that he owned many slaves, that he owned or claimed many thousands of acres of land, and that he was held in high esteem by his contemporaries. To understand the economic and social trajectory of Verdura, and, by extrapolation, archaeological expectations manifested in the cultural remains, the following questions are addressed: How did the economic and social status of Verdura's owners compare to other plantation owners in Florida? Did Verdura's status as an "elite" plantation remain unchanged or did it diminish through time? Did life at Verdura reflect the general economic decline of the Cotton Kingdom?

The status of a plantation would be determined according to several factors: the number of slaves owned by the planter, the amount of land owned, the agricultural production in crops and livestock, and the social and political status of the plantation owner. Since the situation of any given plantation was subject to change on an almost daily basis, and that change was dependent on so many variables, the status of a plantation or of its owner would have reflected a constantly fluid, not static, state. The complications of classifying the status of nineteenth century plantations, as discussed in an article included in *Approaches to Material Culture Research for Historical Archaeologists* by William Adams and Sarah Jane Boling, are summarized below.

Early attempts at status classifications were based primarily on the number of slaves held by the planter. Adams and Boling cite three studies in which the level of a high status planter was indicated: David Hundley, 1860, states that you were a Southern Gentleman (high status) if you owned 50 or more slaves; Ulrich Phillips, 1929, uses 20 or more slaves as an indicator of high status; and Herbert Weaver, 1945, also uses 50+ as an indicator of the "Big Planter."

118

Later classifications included both number of slaves and land ownership. It was argued, however, that some large land owners had few slaves and, conversely, there were some owners with large slave holdings but little land. Furthermore, planters with large land holdings might have had extensive acreage in swamps, forests, and unimproved land in addition to, but sometimes instead of, pastures and cultivated fields.

Using the number of slaves as the criterion for determining status has its shortcomings. The demographic distribution of the slave community on a given plantation would have had a bearing on a planter's status. A slave population comprised of young adult males would have indicated a higher productivity level than one comprised of aging slaves or one with a high number of women and children. Adams and Boling caution that if one uses slave ownership as the primary indicator of planter status, it is also necessary to consider which type of labor, gang or task system, was in use. It would also be helpful to know if the planter hired out or rented his slaves; some who might have done so might have had little land but a relatively good financial situation from their investment in human property. (There is some indication that Chaires hired out his slaves, at least for public works, but the system of labor he used is not known.)

In Florida in 1850, there were 3,520 slave owners. Of these, only 134 or 3% owned 50 or more slaves. In 1850 the number of slaves in Florida ranged from 1 for 699 slave owners to a high of one owner with 300 to 499 slaves.

If the classification of Verdura as an elite plantation is based strictly on slave numbers, it could be said that it was indeed of an elite, upper class status. From the time Benjamin Chaires became established in Leon County, he had more than 50 slaves, and Verdura would have been included in the three percent of Florida plantation owners in 1850 with 50 or more slaves. The "over 50" ranking continued until the end of the Civil War, although slave ownership for thirteen of those years was shared by Charles Powell and Thomas Butler.

119

Slaves and Acreage for Arbitrary Years at Verdura

Who	Year	Acres	# Slaves
Benjamin	1829	9,400	107
Benjamin	1838	9,440	80
Benjamin & Sarah's estates	1846	720	229
Charles & Thomas	1850	720	126
Charles & Thomas	1859	920	151
Charles & Thomas	1861	1,000	91
Charles & Thomas	1863	1,000	93

Adams and Boling state, "The economic control which can be brought to bear, not ownership, provides the relative economic status or worth. Land control is as important as landownership as a socio-economic variable." In Leon County in 1829, there were 13 planters with over 1,000 acres; there were 50 in 1839 and 70 in 1860. The average acreage of large properties in Leon County was 2,208 in 1839 and 2,432 in 1860. This would place the Verdura acreage well above the county average the year after Chaires's death (1839), but below average by 1860. Even if the ownership of Charles Powell's and Thomas Butler's other plantations is taken into account, they would have owned around 2,000 acres each, including Verdura. Thus, their individual total land ownership was somewhat below average in 1860. Using land ownership alone as a criterion for status evaluation would take Verdura out of the ranks of the elite by 1860.

During the 1870s, with the advent of tenant farming and the overall economic decline in cotton farming, Verdura became heavily mortgaged. Charles Powell's "economic control" of the land, to which Adams and Boling refer, became almost nonexistent at Verdura. One cannot maintain economic control over land which, for all practical purposes, creates indebtedness to another party.

Another way of looking at the status of a plantation is to investigate its agricultural output. Little is known about the amount of cotton or other crops that were produced at Verdura during Benjamin Chaires's lifetime, but one could assume, given his wealth and acreage, that it was fairly prodigious. In 1839, the brig "Chairs [*sic*]" left St. Marks for New York with 432 bales of cotton. That year there were at least three Chaires plantations (Verdura and the plantations of Benjamin's brothers Thomas Peter and Green Hill), so the cotton may have come from any or all three. Clifton Paisley sets an arbitrary figure of two hundred bales as the measure of a major cotton producer. By 1860, according to Paisley's assessment, only two Chaires family members, Joseph Chaires, son of Benjamin, and his cousin Green A. Chaires, produced 200 or more bales of cotton. Notably absent from the list are Charles Powell and Thomas Butler, who produced only 150 bales between them—not major players in Leon County's cotton production.

The final indication of the status of a plantation lies in the social and political standing of the owner himself. There is no doubt that Benjamin Chaires was held in high esteem by his contemporaries in business and in politics. This is reflected in his repeated nominations to positions of influence, as recorded in the Territorial Papers, and in the leadership he commanded in public works projects, such as the building of the early railroads and in the establishment of the banking industry. Although Charles Powell appears to have been active in some local organizations and served for one session in the state legislature, neither he nor Thomas Butler (nor their siblings) ever attained the prominence or level of respect held by their father.

Did Verdura fit the definition of an "elite" plantation? During the time of Benjamin Chaires, it was decidedly so. He owned over 50 slaves, he was the owner of almost 10,000 acres of land in Leon County over which he had complete economic control, the agricultural output of his land was believed to have been considerable, and he was a man of influence and social standing. During the Civil War, around 90 slaves worked for

Verdura's owners (as well at two other plantations), and the property consisted of 1,000 acres. Agricultural production was below that of a large operation, and neither owner was particularly noted for leadership in community or state affairs. By the 1870s, there were no slaves to provide substantial personal worth, and the owned acreage was below the county average. Charles Powell's economic control over the land was decreasing due to mortgages, and agricultural production was sparse. After 1881, the year of Charles's death, heavy mortgage debt and court costs consumed whatever profit there might have been from dwindling agricultural production. Economic control was lost, the owners had little or no social or political status, acreage was sold to satisfy debts, and there was no human property. While Verdura began as an elite, upper class operation, it saw a steady decline over the 79 years of Chaires ownership. This social and economic decline at Verdura was a microcosm of the fate of the Cotton Kingdom throughout the old South: no more free labor meant greater expense growing cotton and other crops, which meant a person's net worth was less, which in turn affected the ability to obtain credit. This change in economic status should be clearly visible in Verdura's archaeological record. *

My Master's thesis was completed in 2001 and was entitled The Verdura Place: A Historical Overview and Preliminary Archaeological Survey. *Much of the material for this book, particularly the post-Benjamin Chaires ownership and the African-American presence at Verdura comes from the thesis, and was completed with the cooperation of The St. Joe Company, which has owned Verdura since 1948. Upon completion, I presented St. Joe with two copies of that thesis.*

CHAPTER 8
The Youngest Son

Charles Powell Chaires, youngest son of Benjamin Chaires, was born in 1830 in Florida, in Leon County. (He may have been named for his mother's brother, Charles Powell, or his father's brother Charles with his mother's maiden name as his middle name.) Charles was eight years old when his father died, and he was to become the owner of Verdura until his death in 1881. Most of the land would remain a part of his estate until it was declared insolvent in 1896. His significance to the story of Benjamin Chaires developed from a family scandal of which Charles was a central figure, and which led to the end of the Chaires's possession of their ancestral lands.

On May 25, 1846, eight years after his father's death and the year his mother died, Charles's inheritance was placed under the guardianship of his older brothers Joseph, Green D., and Furman Chaires, until he was to reach lawful age in 1851. The 1850 Census shows that Charles shared a domicile with his next oldest brother, Thomas Butler, who was two years his senior; it is presumed that they lived together at Verdura until about 1851 (and possibly longer), the year of Charles Powell's first marriage. The two brothers were linked together in almost all of their personal and business transactions for the duration of their lives. Each inherited land from their father: Charles was to become the owner of Ever May, a plantation of about 1,000 acres only a few miles northwest of Verdura, and Thomas was master of Tiger Tail, located due north of Verdura.

On April 30, Charles married Sarah Ann (or Sallie) Raines in Thomas County, Georgia, where she had been born on September 16, 1832. She appears rarely in the public records. On November 28, 1857 Sarah's name was included on a deed for land that Charles sold to Benjamin Stephens, and she is listed on the 1860 Leon County census. A year of death, 1866, was found, but was not supported by other documentation. It is apparent that she died after July 21, 1860 (the day the census was taken), and before July 23, 1867, when Charles remarried. She is presumed to be buried in the family graveyard at Verdura, but there is no grave marker for her there, and there are no records of any children born to her.

Charles was a respected member of the community. In 1851, he served as secretary of the Southern Rights Association of Roache's Crossroad and Natural Bridge, an organization formed as sectional difficulties developed along with fears over the future of slavery. In 1854, he served as a juror in the Leon County Circuit Court, and he was a state legislator representing Leon County from November 1856 to January 1857. Some of the laws enacted during the session addressed issues which included sales of public lands, auctioneers, ferries, the telegraph, land for railroads and schools, and various county issues, but the rising controversy over slavery occupied an increasing amount of the legislature's time: laws requiring better patrolling, guardians for Free Negroes, the better government of slaves in Monroe County, the prevention of slaves from hiring their own time, and the prevention of slaves trading with free persons of color in Florida without the consent of a guardian. The session also provided legislation for people to change names, for the establishment of new counties and county seats, for new banks, and there were various monetary appropriations. Charles was paid $107.00 for his service during the session. In 1860, as secession loomed, Charles attended the Democratic meeting as a representative from Natural Bridge to select delegates for the State Convention. He was also chosen to represent Leon County at the State Democratic Convention in April.

Verdura, Ever May, and Cedar Keys

The 1860 census for Leon County shows two entries for Charles. The value of Charles Powell's personal property in the first entry, which would have included slave holdings, was $58,000. The second entry shows his personal property worth $5,000.00. In this census, the ages given for Charles and his wife are incorrect. He is listed as being 34 years of age when he was actually 30, and his wife Sarah is listed as being 25 when she actually was 28.

Based upon their activities before, during, and immediately after the Civil War, it appears that the brothers inherited their father's inclination for business risk. In May of 1858 the brothers bought out their siblings' interest in Verdura and the following October put the plantation up for sale with an advertisement in the Tallahassee *Floridian and Journal* of October 2nd.

> ...the undersigned offer for sale their plantation known as Verdura, situated about nine miles East of Tallahassee and lying between the Pensacola and Georgia and St. Marks and Tallahassee Railroad within five miles of either road, and containing 920 acres, or thereabouts 500 of which is cleared. The lands are as good as any in the county, the location healthy and the water the best this side of the mountains. Upon the premises is a GOOD BRICK DWELLING, three stories high, and containing thirteen large rooms. The outhouses are of Brick and built in the most substantial manner.

The brothers might have had plans to relocate because by 1861, Charles Powell, along with brothers Thomas Butler and Green D., appear on the Levy County tax rolls. They owned town lots in Cedar Keys, which was located on the island known as Atsena Otie, a short distance by water from the present town of Cedar Key. The original Cedar Keys was destroyed by a hurricane and tidal wave in 1896, but the remains of some of the buildings can still be seen along with the old town cemetery. There is some indication that the brothers invested in "vessels" and owned plantations in the area. They may have also been involved in timber harvesting. Around 1863, according to Jerrell Shofner, "C.P. Chaires was cutting timber at Cedar Key when

Confederate officials ordered all civilians out of the area. He returned to his Leon County plantation and lived without incident until 1865." Charles became Power of Attorney for Charles W. Johnson of Atsena Otie in February of 1866. It appears that Mr. Johnson defaulted on the mortgage on a mill, but was not able to pay it off. He appointed Charles to take over his business interest in the mill and get his affairs in order. In 1870, Charles was appointed a Road Commissioner in Levy County, but by 1871, all established road districts were abolished and new commissioners appointed.

Charles and his brother Thomas Butler formed business firms during their years at Cedar Keys. They were variously referred to as C.P. and T.B. Chaires, Chaires & Co., C.P. Chaires & Co., and T.B. Chaires & Co. On November 14, 1862, the brothers purchased jointly $1,041^{1/2}$ acres in Levy County. These joint ventures of the brothers in Cedar Keys is somewhat surprising in light of their attempt in 1858 to "bring their joint effort to a close" in their advertisement to sell Verdura. The plantation was not sold, however, and the brothers remained joint owners of it until late in 1877.

Charles appears on the 1870 Levy County census as living with "Mary R," a 28 year old white woman from Georgia who was "keeping house." Charles's second wife, and cousin of his first wife, whom he married on July 23, 1867, in Duncanville, Georgia, was named Martha, also known as Mamie and Mattie. Because the ages are correctly recorded in this census and because Mattie was born in Georgia, it is probable that Mary R was actually Martha and the enumerator of the census was mistaken about her name. Martha was the daughter of Major Jackson J. Mash, a prominent planter from Thomas County who was described as having a "palatial home at old Duncanville, where in antebellum days, as well as since, he dispensed with liberal hand that hospitality which characterized the Southern planter of the olden time." Duncanville was located in the vicinity of the present community of Beachton, Georgia.

With her marriage to Charles Powell, Mattie was transplanted from the socially elite environs of her wealthy father's circle to the rough seacoast town that was Cedar Keys, and to the lonely life of a rural plantation mistress in Leon County—a typical situation for planters' wives in that era. Some planters, like Charles, were involved in businesses beyond the management of their plantations, and their frequent absences from home often put a serious strain on their marriages. Mattie's feelings about her situation are revealed in a letter written later to Charles's brother Green D., in which she says, "I never should have felt so desperately unloved, unappreciated and neglected for so long a time." In 1876, Martha's apparent dissatisfaction with her lonely life in the wilds of Levy and Leon counties took a dramatic turn. In order to understand how this drama unfolded, it is necessary to jump ahead to 1880, the year that Charles Powell Chaires spent incarcerated in the Leon County jail and the year that he petitioned the court to dissolve his marriage to Martha Mash. The following narrative is a synthesis of data compiled from court testimony, personal letters, deed records and Charles's will, all found in the Leon County archives.

A Scandal Revealed

The petition for dissolution of marriage that Charles Powell Chaires presented to the Leon County court in March of 1880 began with a startling charge. He asserted that in January of 1878, he had returned to his Leon County home, Ever May, and discovered that his 35 year old wife of eleven years was pregnant. He had either been absent from her or they had not been intimate for some time, because he knew immediately that the baby she was carrying was not his. When he asked who the father was, she told him that "he knew," but he asserted that he thought her "too pure for anything of this kind." He evicted her from their home the next day and instructed her to return to her father in Thomas County. A month later, she returned unannounced, stating that she wanted to return to Ever May and that she had not told her

127

parents the true reason for her "visit" to Thomas County. Charles took her back to her parents' house and told them of her illicit affair and the pregnancy. In discussing the situation with his father-in-law, Charles stated that he wanted to "do the honorable thing" and then agreed to take Martha with him on the first leg of his upcoming business trip. The plan was for her to give birth to the baby in New Orleans, and place the baby in an "asylum," after which he would take Martha to Tennessee and continue his business trip to Crestline, Ohio. Martha's expenses were to be paid by her father. The trip worked out as planned. A search of orphanage records in New Orleans for that year revealed that one Capt. W.H. Manning found an 18 day old baby whose parents were unknown. The baby was sent to the St.Vincent Infant Orphan Asylum on April 22, 1878. It was the only infant, within the proper time period, found abandoned in New Orleans.

On February 18, before they left on the trip, Charles conveyed in trust to Martha's brother, Henry Terrell Mash, the Burgess Tract at Verdura for Martha's benefit. (Perhaps, if there was an old family house located on the Burgess Tract, Charles imagined it would be a reasonable dwelling place for his errant wife.) On the same day, Benjamin Cadwallader Chaires (Ben C.), Charles's nephew (son of Benjamin Chaires Jr.), relinquished to Mash his one-third interest in a water mill Charles and he recently constructed on Ever May. Income from the mill was to be used for Martha's benefit. The court testimony is unclear as to when Charles found out that his wife's lover was his nephew Ben Cadwallader, but it seems that the transactions were designed to effect an "honorable" means by which her family and her lover would provide for Martha's welfare. Why else would Ben C. have surrendered his share of the mill to Martha's brother?

By the time Charles arrived in Ohio in late May, it is obvious that he was well aware of the adulterer's identity. In a letter to Charles, Martha evidently replied to a comment he made about a visit she might have had from Ben C. in Tennessee: "I can send you a certificate from this family [with whom she was boarding]

128

that he made me no visit while here. It was by a mere accident that I even heard that he was here. If I am not mistaken he only remained one night. If he told Bro. Tom he wanted to see me before leaving Fla [*sic*] he certainly changed his mind." Charles also came to know that the affair had been going on since February of 1876, when court records revealed that "one Benjamin C. Chaires had carnal connections with the said Martha Mash Chaires and she did then and there commit adultery with him."

At some point after Charles made the land transaction with Henry Terrell Mash, he came to the conclusion that Mash had betrayed him. Whether the betrayal had to do with the identity of the adulterer or with some other insult is unclear. He must have told Martha that he expected her to retrieve the deeds because she wrote to his brother Green D. that she could not interfere on the matter of land Charles deeded to her brother because she "knows nothing of the law and its advantages and disadvantages." Later she wrote to Charles that she wanted to be able to return to their marriage so she would try to get the titles back from her brother "if I have to go to Albany [Georgia] to get them." This evidently never happened. In his will, Charles complained that, "This re-conveyance deed, from Mattie M. Chaires to me, was stolen by her, on my way home to Florida, and [*sic*] I was bringing her to her father. I think it was stolen in Cincinati [*sic*], where she wanted to remain."

Like Father, Like Son

In the years leading up to and including the time that this domestic upheaval was taking place, Charles began to set the stage for the eventual, though unintentional, financial collapse of his estate. In 1870, he had secured a loan from Earle and Perkins of New York City with a mortgage on his plantation, Ever May. In 1873 he secured a debt owed to his nephew, the future adulterer Benjamin Cadwallader, by signing over Ever May and seven mules to Benjamin for his use and profit. In 1874, he and

Thomas Butler (under the firm name T.B. and C.P. Chaires) secured a loan from Earle and Perkins with a mortgage on Verdura, less three acres for the graveyard of which Benjamin Chaires's grave was the center. In December of 1877 and in February of 1878, Thomas Butler gave over his share of Verdura to Charles so that the loan agreement could be rewritten with Charles holding title to the plantation. In January of 1878, Charles "bought" Ever May back from Benjamin Cadwallader for $10.00 and was also able to retrieve three of his mules. At that time he also borrowed $450.00 from his niece Octavia, Benjamin Cadwallader's sister, for construction expenses on the mill at Ever May and secured the loan with 80 acres of Ever May land.

At the same time that Charles was incurring debt, he was also buying and selling property. Around 1859 Benjamin Jr. was having marital problems with his wife and, in an effort to keep her from acquiring Fauntleroy, he attempted to sell the property he had inherited from his father. The plantation stayed in the family, however, as it was conveyed to brother Furman. After Furman's death, Charles became administrator of his estate and, in 1870, attempted to purchase Fauntleroy in trust for Benjamin Jr.'s children Octavia and Benjamin Cadwallader. This effort was blocked by Furman's widow and the transaction halted by litigation for several years. The Fauntleroy deeds were finally conveyed to Benjamin Cadwallader in trust to nephew Samuel Parkhill Chaires for Octavia in January of 1878.

The Scandal Escalates

Charles returned from his trip to Ohio in early October of 1878. The public records do not reveal much activity for him in the months immediately following his return, other than his attempt to collect payment for the sale of a mule in January of 1879. Perhaps his business dealings in Cedar Keys kept his attention drawn in that direction rather than to his interests in Leon County. Later in the year, however, he was in Leon County and on November 8, 1879, he wrote his will. It seems that he wrote it knowing that his life might soon be in jeopardy. On November 17, in downtown Tallahassee, he and his nephew Benjamin Cadwallader Chaires engaged in what the *Weekly Floridian* referred to as a "shooting affray.":

> Yesterday, on Munroe [*sic*] street [*sic*], an encounter occurred between Ben C. Chaires and C.P. Chaires, in which several shots were exchanged, resulting in the wounding of the former in the left leg below the hip. The encounter was the result of a feud of long standing, growing out of domestic troubles. Mr. Chaires's wound is not considered a dangerous one. Both parties were promptly arrested, which, perhaps, prevented more bloodshed.

On November 18, the Grand Jury indicted both men for "carrying secret arms" and Charles was indicted for "assault with intent to murder." After refusing to "give bond," Charles was imprisoned in the Leon County Jail where he remained until December 4, 1880, when three associates put up bond so that he could be free until the final disposition of the case scheduled for the third Monday in March of 1881. In that disposition, made on March 21, the indictments for carrying secret arms were transferred to the Leon County Justice of the Peace, and Charles's indictment for assault with intent to murder was ordered *nol pros:* a decision rendered by the prosecutor that there would be no further intent to pursue a conviction in the case.

On the same day that the assault charges against him were dropped, Martha responded, in the Judge's chambers, to Charles's accusations of adultery by stating that she told him she was pregnant in September of 1877, that she lived with him executing her wifely duties until after the birth of the child, and that on his return from Ohio in the Fall of 1878, he "kept himself aloof from her." She offered no explanation of what happened to

131

the baby or why, if it had been a legitimate child, she would have left it in New Orleans. In May of that year, Charles testified that they had lived apart since January 2nd or 3rd of 1878, and the cause was "her adultery with Ben C. Chaires at my residence on the May Plantation in this county." He claimed that she confessed everything. Court was adjourned until the first week of June, but additional records from this case were not found, and there was no judgment made in the case prior to the mysterious death of Charles Powell at the St. Marks Lighthouse in Wakulla County on August 17, 1881.

An undocumented family story indicates that Charles died of yellow fever, but this same story is full of inconsistencies and inaccuracies, so the cause of death, while within the realm of possibility, is not conclusive. His obituary did not appear in the local paper, *Land of Flowers*, until October, cites an incorrect date of death, and offers no cause of death. It is known from the probate records that the executors of his estate paid lighthouse keepers Breen and Dent $12.00 for "attention to Mr. Chaires" on August 21, and on August 22, they paid Simon Hawkins $1.00 for "hunting horse" (probably Tallaho). A payment of $2.00 to Mr. Ben Stephens for "taking up horse" was made on August 26, 1881. Charles Powell Chaires is said to be buried in the family graveyard at Verdura, but his grave marker, if there ever was one, is not visible today.

End Game

Charles did not include his estranged wife in his will, which was probated on August 29, 1881. Since he had no children, he left portions of his estate, which included land in Leon and Levy counties plus his share of his father's estate, to various nieces and nephews. Verdura was left to Green D.'s oldest son, Samuel Parkhill Chaires, "in trust, for other sons not including his son Bradford, but he can use the revenue from said place for the education of his daughters, as well as his sons, until his sons become of age." In addition to his instructions to leave certain parcels of property to his nieces and nephews, he also wanted his executors to "pay over to Fred Towle, Myers Ormand Chaires and Laurence Harley, in trust for the City of Tallahassee, one hundred dollars annually untill [sic] five hundred dollars are paid for the purpose of founding and establishing a Public Library."

On September 10th, an appraisal of Charles's personal property was conducted. With the exception of some silver spoons which were family heirlooms, his belongings were quite modest. The list included common household and kitchen furniture, bedding, farm implements, eight mules, one horse (named Tallaho) and a revolver. The total appraised value was $1,008.60. The estate sale was held on January 14, 1882, with most buyers members of the family. The sale brought in $1,090.05.

In April of 1882, Martha Mash presented her first petition for dower against Charles's estate. This would have included one-third of her husband's real estate, which amounted to 306 $^{2/3}$ acres of Verdura plus land at Ever May. She was eventually also awarded half of the rents paid by tenant farmers on both properties. The executors of Charles Powell's will made every attempt to keep her from acquiring any land or money from his estate, but in the end they failed. No one except Martha and Benjamin Cadwallader (who refused to testify) had first-hand knowledge of their affair. Samuel Parkhill Chaires testified that Charles had told him about his domestic troubles, that Martha had not been living at Ever May since Charles's return from Ohio, and that he knew personally that Ben C. Chaires lived at Fauntleroy, only a little over a mile from Charles's place, and often went to Ever May to tend to the mules. All was considered hearsay and was not enough to convince the court to refuse Martha her widow's due. When Samuel's testimony failed to convince the court, the executors petitioned to have the estate declared insolvent. Mortgagees threatened foreclosure, which precipitated an injunction against the sale of any portions of Charles's estate and caused further delays in coming to a resolution.

133

The final disposition in the matter of Martha's dower took place in Live Oak, Florida, on January 4, 1896, when the judge ruled that Martha's plea for dower was legitimate and that it took precedence over the insolvency of her husband's estate. That decision also rejected a claim by mortgage holder Robert Munro that he could collect a balance on the mortgage left from 1891. Almost fifteen years after the death of her estranged husband, Martha was free to sell the land she acquired from the estate of Charles Powell Chaires. Martha sold her parcels on Ever May and Verdura to Robert W. Williams, and Tallahassee mortgage holder Robert Munro acquired the remaining Verdura acreage. These sales brought to an end the ownership of the Verdura Place by the Chaires family. The Verdura site was eventually purchased by the St. Joe Paper Company around 1948.

Benjamin Cadwallader Chaires died on April 29, 1909, and was buried at St. John's Episcopal Church Cemetery. He was the father of five children and was a respected member of the community, who served in the Florida Legislature in 1897.

Ben C. Chaires in the 1897 Florida Legislature.
Photo courtesy of the State Archives of Florida, Florida
Memory, http://floridamemory.com/items/show/32308

Martha died on November 2, 1911, in Thomasville, Georgia, after marrying her sister's widower, William Frank Thomas, in 1906. She had worked as a "matron of sanitation" and was a landlady for three properties in Thomasville at the time of her death. In her will, she requested that her body "be buried in a decent and Christian-like manner suitable to my circumstances and condition in life." While other members of her family and her second husband are buried in the Laurel Hill Cemetery in Thomasville, Martha's modest gravestone resides in a solitary corner of the Ochlocknee Baptist Church graveyard in Beachton, Georgia.

EPILOGUE

Post-Chaires Ownership of Verdura

In 1890, when mortgager Robert J. Munro took ownership of the Verdura property and with the sale of Martha's Verdura acreage to her attorney Robert W. Williams, the Chaires family lost control of the land they had managed to retain since Benjamin's death in 1838. The part of the property which included the mansion house ruins eventually was sold to Dr. O.W. Britt, and land north of the house, which included the clay pits, was purchased by Gordon Pichard.

After World War II, the St. Joe Paper Company increased their land holdings for the purpose of farming slash pine trees for harvest to send to their newly built paper and pulp mills, the closest of which was located at Port St. Joe, Florida. In 1947, the Henderson family, descendants of Benjamin Chaires through his daughter Sarah Jane Ward, sold their South Wood Farm to the paper company. This acquisition added to St. Joe's vast acreage all over the state of Florida and in the southeastern part of Leon County. In 1948, St. Joe's additional purchases in southeast Leon County included the Verdura parcels.

Thoughts on Benjamin Chaires's Lost Legacy

Citizens of Leon County, Florida, are quite familiar with the Chaires name in general and with Benjamin Chaires as a local historical figure. Indeed, there is a road named for him in the eastern part of the county. His untimely death at age 52, however, brought an end to his many civic ventures and memories of those projects were soon lost to the fog of time. The Lake Wimico/Iola Railroad, of which he was so proud and to which he fully committed himself, failed soon after his death when the railroad foundered and no longer served the City of St. Joseph. All equipment and land belonging to the railroad was

137

sold off to regain Chaires's monetary investments in the company.

Chaires's involvement with the establishment of banks in Middle Florida was undermined by the dubious patronage system of awarding privileges to the wealthy and politically connected. In 1837, the year before Chaires's death, the banks began to decline, and the Central Bank, of which he was president, was later subsumed by the Union Bank under the direction of son Joseph Chaires. His largest single land purchase, the Alachua Lands, was tied up in district and federal courts for fifty-three years. The outcome was that the land was never conveyed to Chaires's descendants, but his estate was issued scrip to be used to obtain acreage of "public" lands wherever they could be found and were not necessarily contiguous acres. His East Florida lands were sold off in the 1870s because without slavery, legal heirs could not afford to work the land. And, having been one of the greatest of cotton producers in Middle Florida, crop and cotton yields on his plantations were later much reduced without the free labor provided by slaves prior to the War. Chaires's palatial mansion, thought to be the grandest in all of Middle Florida, burned in the 1880s, never to be lived in again, and, after many years of legal wrangling, the Chaires family lost this most prized piece of inherited real estate.

Chaires's name is known, one of his plantations is known, but much of his history and contributions to the development of trade in the area have been forgotten. The single tangible artifact left to us that came directly from his hands, are the bricks he had fabricated for numerous building projects: The Columns, the Mount Vernon arsenal in Chattahoochee, the second building used as the state capital, and of course, the building remains at Verdura. Our final, touchable symbol of Chaires's place in Florida history comes to us from the work of slaves, to whom he owed a great debt of gratitude for helping him become "Florida's first millionaire," his seemingly most well-known, if unverifiable, achievement.

APPENDIX

Notes on the Ancestry
and
Family of Benjamin Chaires

Ancestry Chart

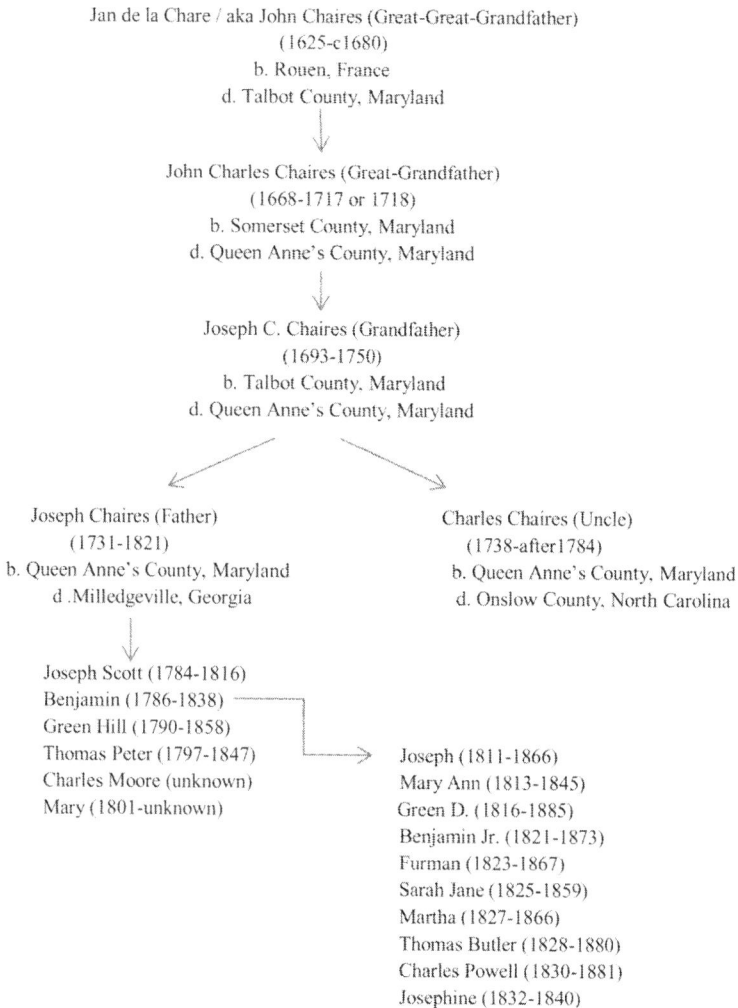

Jan de la Chare / aka John Chaires (Great-Great-Grandfather)
(1625-c1680)
b. Rouen, France
d. Talbot County, Maryland

↓

John Charles Chaires (Great-Grandfather)
(1668-1717 or 1718)
b. Somerset County, Maryland
d. Queen Anne's County, Maryland

↓

Joseph C. Chaires (Grandfather)
(1693-1750)
b. Talbot County, Maryland
d. Queen Anne's County, Maryland

Joseph Chaires (Father)
(1731-1821)
b. Queen Anne's County, Maryland
d. Milledgeville, Georgia

Charles Chaires (Uncle)
(1738-after1784)
b. Queen Anne's County, Maryland
d. Onslow County, North Carolina

Joseph Scott (1784-1816)
Benjamin (1786-1838)
Green Hill (1790-1858)
Thomas Peter (1797-1847)
Charles Moore (unknown)
Mary (1801-unknown)

Joseph (1811-1866)
Mary Ann (1813-1845)
Green D. (1816-1885)
Benjamin Jr. (1821-1873)
Furman (1823-1867)
Sarah Jane (1825-1859)
Martha (1827-1866)
Thomas Butler (1828-1880)
Charles Powell (1830-1881)
Josephine (1832-1840)

Sarah Powell Chaires

Wife of Benjamin Chaires
(1790–1846)

Children: Joseph
Mary Ann
Green D.
Benjamin, Jr.
Furman
Sarah Jane
Martha
Thomas Butler
Charles Powell
Josephine

OBITUARY

The Florida *Sentinel*
March 17, 1846

Departed this life on the 12th instant, in the 56th year of her age,
at her residence in the country,

Mrs. SARAH CHAIRES,
relict of the late Major Benjamin Chaires.

In the death of this excellent and exemplary lady society has been deprived of a valuable and useful member. To her bereaved children, nothing can repair the loss they have sustained. As a mother, she was kind, affectionate and devoted; instructing her children by precept and example in all that was useful in private life, and calculated to make them respectable and honorable members of the community in which they live. As a friend, she was true and faithful; as a mistress, she was kind, careful and humane, ministering to all the wants of her servants in sickness, and attending to their comfortable conditions in health. As a Christian she was modest and unobtrusive, though firm and decided. She was unable to attend the public worship of God, from her increasing infirmities, for several years; yet she worshipped in the secret sanctuary of the closet, and He, in whom she had put her trust and served in life, manifested his power and his presence in death; she died happy, in view of the bright and blessed immortality which remains to the people of God.

EPITAPH

Sacred to the Memory
of
Sarah
wife of
Ben Chaires
Born 17th of September 1790
Died 12th of March 1846
45 years 5 months
and 26 days
Lo I come to do thy will O God.
Heb. 10 Chap.V.

Her unmeasured devotion to her children
Can never be forgotten by them.

BURIAL

Verdura Plantation

Joseph Chaires
(1811–1866)

Plantation: Lake Como (near Rose)
Only child: Charles Robert Chaires

<u>TIMELINE</u>

1811   Joseph born in Baldwin County, GA – Dec. 25

1824   Future 2nd wife Polly Ann Chaires born

1833   Conveys to Joseph and Green Hill in trust for Mary Ann
        slaves, horse, barouche & harness for her use and NOT
        for her husband's – April 9

1835   Joseph enlists in Mounted Volunteers, Florida Militia for
        five weeks

183?   Joseph was a director of the Union Bank in Tallahassee
        until its collapse in 1838 and then promoted the charter
        of the Bank of the State of Florida

1839   Joseph marries Russell Ormand – July 7

        Joseph places notice in the *Florida Herald* warning
        trespassers not to go onto the lands of his father's estate
        in East Florida: the Plain and Swamp of San Diego,
        Chacarras, General Savannah, Beach Plantation on
        Amelia Island, 4,500 acres on the River Halifax and
        200 acres held in common with Thomas Butler on the
        Plains and Swamp of Diego (plus others totaling 9,355
        acres in St. Johns and Mosquito counties) – August 29

1841   Joseph sells to Robert Berry horse, mules, land on
        promissory note – April 1

Russell Ormand and sister Helen die during Yellow Fever epidemic – Aug. 27 & 29; buried at Verdura

1842   Joseph holds slave auction at Fauntleroy to pay off his father's mortgage owed Robert Berry

1843   Joseph's gin-house was blown away and with it 30,000 pounds of cotton and five bales just packed – Sept. 27

1844   Joseph marries his cousin Polly Green Chaires – May 28 (she was the daughter of his Uncle Tom Peter Chaires)

1845   Joseph appeals to the Supreme Court to allow a hearing on a change in the survey of the Alachua lands; he lost the appeal – January term

1846   Joseph petitions the Senate re the Alachua survey; goes to Committee on the Judiciary – Feb. 9

Senate refers bill (S. 86) for the relief of Joseph Chaires to Committee on the Judiciary – March 25

Furman, Joseph and Green are appointed guardians of Thomas, Charles and Martha – May 25

1850   Joseph and Green granted charter for Plank Road Company (to be built from Newport to Thomasville)

Joseph purchases two lots at Sulphur Springs in Magnolia – Nov. 11

1855   Joseph promoted the charter of the Bank of the State of Florida

1857   Only child Charles Robert born – date unknown

1858   Joseph sells his share of Verdura to Charles and Thomas – May 18

1859 Petition of Joseph Chaires, executor of B. Chaires, referred to the Committee on Private Land Claims (Journal of the Senate) – Dec. 27

1860 Joseph declines to be trustee for Ben Burgess's estate; Green D. accepts – July 17

1866 Joseph dies – April 28; buried at Verdura

OBITUARY

The *Semi-Weekly Floridian*
May 11, 1866

DIED, at his residence, in this county, on the 28th April after a lingering and painful illness, JOSEPH CHAIRES, Esq., in the fifty-fifth year of his age.

Mr. Chaires was one of our oldest citizens, having come to Florida with his father shortly after the exchange of flags. There was no enterprise of a public character to which he was not willing to contribute, for the benefit of his fellow citizens. Although retiring in his habits he always felt a deep interest in whatever promised to promote the public good. The estimation in which he was held by his fellow-citizens was frequently manifested by their repeated calls on him to permit his name to be used (?) as a candidate for the Legislature, but he invariably declined all public honors, content to do all the good he could in the private walks of life. The hospitality of his home was proverbial, and the generosity with which he supplied the wants and relieved the distresses of the poor, made them feel that he was indeed a friend from whose door they would never be turned away. Those who have enjoyed his kindness may well mourn the loss of a benefactor and friend whose liberal hand was ever opened and whose heart ever responded to the demands of friendship and the calls of distress.

To his wife and child he always exhibited an affection to them ?? that was repaid by a devotion which made his domestic life peculiarly one of contentment and peace.

He bore his affliction with exemplary resignation and patience, and his last moments attested that his trust for the present and the future was in the ?? of his crucified Lord.

EPITAPH

IN
MEMORY
OF
JOSEPH CHAIRES
WHO WAS
Born the 25th
Dec. 1811
& died the 28th
April 1866

THIS MONUMENT IS
ERECTED BY HIS WIFE
Blessed are the dead
Who die in the Lord

BURIAL

Verdura Plantation

DEATHS

The Florida Sentinel
September 3, 1841

At the residence of Mr. Jos. Chaires in this county, on the 27th, Miss Ellen Ormond.--------On the 30th, Mrs. Russell Ormond, wife of Mr. Joseph Chaires.

EPITAPH

SACRED
TO THE MEMORY OF
RUSSEL [*sic*] CHAIRES
WHO DEPARTED THIS LIFE
ON THE 29 DAY OF AUGUST AD 1841
AGED 25 YEARS 2 MONTHSAND 20 DAYS
All that heart could wish SHE WAS

EPITAPH

IN MEMORY OF
POLLY GREEN CHAIRES
RELICT OF THE LATE
JOSEPH CHAIRES
WHO DIED ON THE
20th DAY OF MARCH 1870
IN THE 46th YEAR
OF HER AGE

A SINCERE CHRISTIAN EVER MINDFUL
OF HER RELATIONS TO HER GOD,
SHE DIED IN PEACE AND IN THE FULL
HOPE OF A BLESSD IMMORTALITY.
THIS MONUMENT
IS THE LAST TOKEN OF AFFECTION
WHICH AN ONLY CHILD CAN RENDER
TO HER MEMORY.

BURIAL

Old City Cemetery
Tallahassee

Charles R. Chaires (1857 - ??), grandson of Benjamin Chaires
Plantation: Lake Como

1870   Charles R. living with Mariano Papy and family. (Papy
       was executor of Joseph's will.)

1879   Mr. Charles R. Chaires, with his beautiful and
       accomplished wife, has removed to the "Lake Como"
       place about 12 miles east of this city (located at Rose) –
       Sept. 16, *The Weekly Floridian*

1880   Sells 1,878 acres in Wakulla Co. on Wakulla River to
       Ben C. – Jan. 14

1882   Joseph Chaires mansion burns at Lake Como – possibly
       Dec. 10 (may have been Verdura fire – news articles
       conflict with historic documents)

1885   On Leon County census: Charles R. (28), wife Martha
       (24), daughters Annie (6) and Olga M. (4)

1889   Charles sells Lake Como and moves out of state – April

BURIAL

Unknown

A FIRE

The Weekly Floridian
Dec. 19, 1882

The fine old mansion of the late Joseph Chaires, ten miles
east of Tallahassee, the property of his only heir, Charles R.
Chaires, was destroyed by fire one day last week. This was one

of the largest and handsomest of the old-time palatial residences built in this favored region of Florida in the prosperous antebellum times.

The fire was first discovered in the upper part of the building about two o'clock in the afternoon, and in a short time the grand old mansion was entirely destroyed. Most of the furniture was saved. No insurance.

Thus in a few short hours one of the old landmarks of better days in Middle Florida, upon which thousands of dollars was expended, is swept away by devouring flames and nothing but ashes and charred debris remain to mark the site of the once grand old mansion, a monument to the prosperous days of Middle Florida – days forever gone, but still revered in the memory of all Floridians.

Land of Flowers
Dec. 23, 1882

Residence of Charles R. Chaires, nine mi south of the city, was destroyed last week by fire. The accident occurred about midday and most of the furniture was saved. The building had been the old family mansion and was prized on that account. No insurance.

The Weekly Floridian
Dec. 26, 1882

Mr. Charles R. Chaires, whose fine residence on the Lake Como place, 10 miles east of Tallahassee was recently destroyed by fire, will rebuild at once.

Mary Ann Chaires Burgess
(1813 – 1845)

Children: Benjamin Chaires Burgess
            William Gaither Burgess, Jr.

TIMELINE

1813   Mary Ann born – June 6 in GA

1831   Mary Ann marries William Gaither Burgess – May 12

        Wm. Burgess buys land in T1R1, NW, Sec. 28 & 29
        plus 3 city lots – Dec. 20

1832   Benjamin Chaires Burgess born – Aug. 8

        Wm. Burgess buys Lot #118 in city addition – Aug. 23

        Ben sells city lots and land in T1R1, NW to Wm.
        Burgess – May 23

1833   William sells lots 95 & 96 in city to pay debts –
        March 10

        Mary Ann relinquishes claim to dower – March 13

        Chaires conveys to son Joseph and brother Green Hill in
        trust for Mary Ann slaves, horse, barouche & harness for
        her use and NOT for her husband's – April 9

        Ad placed for Marshall's sale of Wm. Burgess' goods –
        May 22

        Marshall's sale at the store of Wm. Burgess (to pay his
        many debts) – June 24

Wm. Burgess brings suit against Berry and Baltzell and some creditors (his creditors and loan security included Chaires and Green Hill) – Oct. 9

Mary Ann moves to New Orleans – Dec. 27 and takes with her Negro woman Sally and child Kitty Ann, 4 years old. Joseph and Green give her permission to take them as "house and waiting maid." Isaac Preston is to oversee the slaves in NO and make sure Wm. Burgess derives no benefit from them or tries to sell them.

1834   William Gaither Burgess Jr. born in New Orleans – Feb. 27

1838   Benjamin Chaires dies – Oct. 4 – and leaves Mary Ann $10,000 for her but not for her husband. She is not included as an heir to any of his land holdings.

William Burgess Jr. dies – Oct. 6 and is buried at Verdura

1840   Joseph and Green go to court to prevent William from getting any inheritance or land. He must promise to live apart from Mary Ann and not to molest her, and has to give up custody of Ben to Mary Ann, Green and Joseph until Ben is 21. Nor can he benefit from any inheritance that Ben might get from Mary Ann. She gives up right to dower and is released of any of his debts. Joseph and Green promise to provide a good, classical education for Benjamin and will pay for it themselves or out of Mary Ann's estate.

1844   William petitions for a replacement of deed that burned in the fire of 1843 for Parts of lots 81 & 82 – May 4 William gives up any claim to Mary Ann's inheritance; it is for her and child Ben only – July 22

1845   Mary Ann dies – Jan. 2

EPITAPH

Sacred to the Memory
Of
Mary Ann
Wife of
William G. Burgess
And daughter of
Benjamin and Sarah Chaires
Born June 6th, 1813
Died January 2, 1845
32 years 6 months and 27 days
[*line illegible due to break in masonry
that was later repaired*]
meek and merciful spirit
and her charitable disposition
knew no bounds
This token
of her worth virtue and long suffering
is erected by her bereaved husband.
Blessed are the pure in heart for they will see God.
Mat. V 8th

BURIAL

Verdura Plantation

EPITAPH

Sacred to the memory of
William Gaither
Son of
William & Mary Ann
Burgess
Born in New Orleans
Feb. 27, 1834
Died Oct. 6, 1838
Suffer the little children to come unto me
and forbid them not for of such
is the Kingdom of Heaven.
Mark C.10 Vi 11

BURIAL

Verdura Plantation

TIMELINE

Benjamin Chaires Burgess (1832-1860), first grandson of
Benjamin Chaires

1860   Doctor visits Ben Burgess from April 26 – July 6.
        Purchase of copious amounts of cod liver oil.

        Benjamin Burgess writes his will and dies at age 28 at
        home of Aunt Martha Gamble; leaves his estate to
        Joseph in trust for his father William and Aunt Martha,
        should she outlive William. Martha is also to get the
        Negro woman Easter and the boy, Dick. The rest is to be
        divided equally, including 20 slaves. Dies July 6 and is
        buried at Verdura. Joseph declines to be executor; Green
        D. becomes executor on July 15. The will is filed July
        28.

The 1860 census was taken on July 7. Ben Burgess is listed as a planter with Real Estate valued at $5,800.00 and personal property at $11,000.00. He was living with W.G. Burgess (father), age 60, his agent, born in NC. Also living with A.W. Boswell, overseer, age 29 from NC who had personal property worth $1,500.00 Ben Burgess's obituary is in the *Floridian and Journal* – July 21

Ben Burgess's estate included fancy and expensive clothing, wine, whiskey, books, chocolates - all purchased on credit. His library was valued at $275.00

1861   Ad in the *Floridian* for auction of S/2 of SE/4 of Sec. 18 (Burgess Tract) – Feb. 18

Charles Powell buys Burgess Tract at auction of Ben Burgess's estate (S/2 of SE/4 of Sec. 18) – May 6

1863   William Burgess writes his will – June 5

1866   William Burgess dies in Levy County at the home of Green D. – end of Oct/early Nov. He leaves his estate to Green D's daughter, Mary Ann, namesake of Burgess's deceased wife. Green is his executor along with William G. Ponder of Thomas County. Will is executed Nov. 2

OBITUARY

Floridian and Journal
July 21, 1860

Died in this city, at the residence of Col. R. H. Gamble, on Friday, the 6th inst., BENJAMIN C. BURGESS, aged 27 years and ten months.

Death is at all times solemn. When it severs the cords that bind old age to life, it is impressive, though expected – When it clips the brittle thread that connects children with earth, it is touching. But when it lays its heavy hand on early manhood and strikes its victim into the tomb, it awakens emotions which nothing else may summon from their slumbering depths. These are indeed the lessons which teach us that man is born to die, and that every pathway in life has its exit at the grave.

The subject of this brief notice possessed those traits of character which endeared him to all who knew him. Retiring in his habits, unobtrusive in his manners and possessing the nicest sensibilities, he was ever keenly alive ? to the feelings of others. His kindness of heart was proverbial, and in its display was the more esteemed because known to be the promptings of a generous nature. Though for some time in feeble health, he little thought, the day before his death, that his life was so near its close. On Thursday, with ??? than his usual cheerfulness, he was engaged in giving directions about his farming interests and on Friday morning his spirit winged its flight from earth. ?? a source of gratification to his friends that on the morning of his death, he ??? his faith in the Savior and his willingness to trust all in Him. As the scenes of life were passing away, and already in the last moments of existence, with still unclouded mind, he ?? all who were near him and especially a young relative at his bedside, to heal ? a wound and ??? ??? ??? we ??? hope that his spirit is at rest with its creator.

EPITAPH

Sacred to the Memory of
Benjamin Chaires Burgess
Born August 8, 1832
Died July 6, 1860

"Yea though I walk through
the valley of the shadow of
death, I will fear no evil;
for thou art with me;
thy rod & thy staff
they comfort me"

TRIBUTE OF RESPECT

At a regular meeting of Leon Lodge, No. 5, L.O.O.F., held on Tuesday evening, July 17th, 1860, the following resolutions were read and adopted:

Whereas Brother B. C. Burgess has been taken from us by the dispensation of our Heavenly Father – therefore,

Resolved, That in the death of brother Burgess our Lodge has sustained the loss of a member who exemplified in his life the teachings of our Order and whose virtues commanded the respect of the old and endeared him to his younger companions; and that we deeply lament the early death of a brother whose social virtues and warm feelings, whose purity of life and conduct and generous sympathies, so well fitted him for illustrating the principles of charity and fraternity.

Resolved, That we tender our sympathy to the father and relatives of our deceased brother.

Resolved, That as a token of respect to our departed brother, the Lodge room be clothed in mourning, that we wear the usual badge of mourning for thirty days, and that a page in the record book be devoted to his memory.

Resolved, That a copy of this resolution be transmitted to the father of the deceased and that they be published in the city papers.   – GEORGE WALTON KNIGHT, Sec'y.

Green D. Chaires
(1816 – 1885)

Plantation: Paisley (?)
Children: Samuel Parkhill Chaires
           Sarah Powell Chaires
           Mary Ann Chaires
           Thomas Peter Chaires
           Martha Jane Chaires
           Joseph George Chaires
           Kate Cocke Chaires
           John Green Chaires
           Agnes Victoria Chaires
           Richard Charles Chaires

1816   Green D. born in GA – Sept. 1

1818   Ann Marie Parkhill, future wife, born – Sept. 29

1840   Green D. marries Ann Maria Parkhill – Jan. 22

1841   Samuel Parkhill Chaires (a son) born – Sept. 12

1846   Furman, Joseph and Green are appointed guardians of Thomas, Charles and Martha – May 25

1850   Joseph and Green D. granted charter for Plank Road Company (to be constructed from Newport to Thomasville)

1854   Green serves as a state legislator in the House from Leon County

1855   Green serves as a state legislator in the House from Leon County

1860   Joseph declines to be trustee for Ben Burgess' estate; Green D. accepts – July 17

1861   Charles, Thomas, Green D. on Levy County tax rolls

Wife Ann Marie Parkhill dies – November 15 and is buried at Verdura

1866   Green D. has a plantation in Levy County, near Jack Ridge, formerly Hinton Place on the Suwannee River; in Mark & Brand index – May 25

William Burgess, brother-in-law, dies in Levy County (at the home of Green D.) – end of Oct/early Nov

1867   Green D. serves as administrator for William Burgess' estate, sues Louis C. Arlidge of Cedar Keys

1869   Samuel Parkhill Chaires marries Mary Catherine "Kate" Hill in Jefferson County – Dec. 8

1870   Wilson A. Barrington on census as working for Green D. Chaires in Leon County

1873   Green D. conveys to Richard C. Chaires, his youngest son, land in T1R2, Sec. 22 – May 26

1878   Martha Mash Chaires writes to Green D. from New Orleans – April

1879   Charles Powell writes his will (bequeaths Verdura to Samuel P. Chaires in trust to use profits for the education of his children); S.P. Chaires is executor – Nov. 8

1881   Green D. serves on the Board of the Leon County
        Schools – Dec.

1882   Green D.'s will indicates Congress is still settling land
        claims in his father's estate

1884   Green D. marries Drucilla Adams (no children) –
        March 6

1885   Green D. dies of possible urinary infection (age 69);
        buried at Verdura – March 1. He was the last of
        Benjamin Chaires's children to die and he was the oldest
        at the time of death.

1920   Drucilla Adams (second wife of Green D. Chaires) dies,
        buried at Crawfordville Cemetery, Crawfordville, FL –
        Jan. 14

OBITUARY

Land of Flowers
11 March 1885

Mr. Green D. Chaires, one of the old settlers of this county, died yesterday at his residence and was buried at the family burying ground ten miles southeast of the city at 12 o'clock today.

GREEN CHAIRES
SEPT. 1. 1816
MARCH 1885

TIMELINE

Samuel Parkhill Chaires (1841 – 1928), grandson of Benjamin Chaires

1861   Samuel Parkhill Chaires and Virginia Alice Bradford married at Verdura

1865   Virginia Alice Chaires writes to her sister that she was able to hear the fighting at Natural Bridge from her home at Verdura; Samuel is in the fight – March 16

1890   Martha Mash files suit against SP Chaires and JA Henderson for rent she was to be paid from land she received as dower for years 1881-84, with interest – January

1906   Samuel Parkhill Chaires applies for Confederate Army pension from Chaires, FL – Oct. 13

1913   Samuel Parkhill Chaires applies for increase in Confederate pension due to disability from "defective vision;" address is Rose, FL

OBITUARY

Tallahassee *Daily Democrat*
Saturday, Dec. 8, 1928

AGED VETERANS PASS OVER RIVER

Mr. Sam J. [*sic*] Chaires, age 88 years of Chaires, Florida, a
native of this section and Confederate Veteran taking active part
in the battle of Natural Bridge, died at his home at Chaires at
midnight, December 8th, after an illness of several weeks. He was
married the first time to Miss Parkhill, and of this union a son
Mr. H.B. Chaires and daughter Mrs. J.H. Patterson, both of
Chaires survive. After the death of his first wife, he was later
married to Miss Kate Hill, and of this union he is survived by the
following children, Mrs. Rosa Ennix of Tallahassee, Mrs. E.L.
Prouse of Jacksonville, Mrs. Chaires Scruggs of Chaires, J.P. and
T.G and Hill Chaires of Chaires. He will be buried in Oakland
cemetery at Tallahassee 3:00 o'clock Sunday afternoon.

[Errors: Samuel's middle name was Parkhill; his first wife was
Virginia Alice Bradford; his mother was Ann Maria Parkhill]

Note: Many descendants of Green D. Chaires are citizens of
Levy County today.

Benjamin Chaires, Jr.
(1821 – 1873)

Plantation: Fauntleroy
Children: Benjamin Cadwallader Chaires
          Octavia Chaires (Greenhow)

TIMELINE

1821   Benjamin Jr. born in GA – Feb. 1 (UGA alum book says born in Leon County, FL)

1844   Ben Jr. marries Mary Shepard – April 30 at St. John's Episcopal Church

1845   Ben Jr. on voter rolls for 1st state election

1846   Ben Jr. owns a $400 lot in town

1847   Benjamin Cadwallader (Ben C.) born – May 14

1848   Ben Jr. serves as juror in Leon County Circuit Court

1849   Ben Jr. serves as juror in Leon County Circuit Court

Octavia born – Jan. 18

1850   Ben Jr. serves as juror in Leon County Circuit Court

Ben Jr. on Democratic committee charged with developing a list of potential candidates for the Legislature and delegates to the state convention – July

1859   Ben Jr. puts Fauntleroy up for sale

Ben Jr. deeds all lands, houses, etc to Ben C and Octavia – June 17

1860   2 Negroes man and girl drowned belonged to Maj. B. Chaires, Jr. flat sank while attempting to cross arm of Lake Lafayette – Jan. 14

Ad appears in Macon *Telegraph* for sale of Fauntleroy – Aug. 27

1863   Mary Shepard sues Ben Jr. for divorce – March 20. They can no longer live together as man and wife. He has kept her from seeing her children, she doesn't know why except he says he doesn't trust her. He testifies that she should not be allowed to influence her children and that she had conspired to have him put in a lunatic asylum. She alleges cruelty.

Ben Jr. and Mary Shepard marriage dissolved – Aug. 15

1864   Ben Jr. and Mary Shepard marriage dissolved – Jan. 8

FL Supreme Court decrees Ben Jr. to pay alimony of $1,000/yr. + $500.00 lawyer's fee – June 22

1865   Ben Jr. is a private in Company C, 5th Florida Battalion Cavalry – Feb. 19

Ben C. takes over at Fauntleroy because of Ben Jr.'s ill health Ben C and Octavia sue their mother to prevent her from selling or removing the slaves Arnold and Fair – Feb. 4

Octavia in school at the Ursuline Convent in Columbia, SC when Sherman on way to GA – Feb

1868   Ben Jr. tried to sell the children's mule, pony, buggy and harness – Dec. 14

[At some point, Ben C. becomes guardian of his mother who had been declared incompetent, a lunatic and an inmate of the Lunatic Asylum of Raleigh, NC]

168

1870   Charles Powell buys land at public sale from Furman's
        estate for Ben C. and Octavia. He was executor of
        Furman's will. Furman came by Fauntleroy when Ben
        Jr. gave it over to him as security on a loan. The property
        was being sold without Ben Jr.'s knowledge (letter to the
        Chancery Court) – March 8
        (Mary S. Chaires was determined to be a "lunatic" and
        was an inmate of the Lunatic Asylum at Raleigh, NC –
        dates unknown)

1873   Benjamin Chaires Jr. dies – April. Site of burial, epitaph,
        obituary unknown or not found.

In 1901 the University of Georgia held a centennial
celebration. For that they published the Centennial Alumni
Catalogue. It solicited information from living alumni, relatives
and friends of all deceased. Ben C. Chaires filled out the
following information on his father, Benjamin Jr.:

> He courted and married to Miss Mary Shepard
> of Tallahassee Fla in 1844. Both parties were of
> rich land and slave owning families. They lived
> many happy years on their landed interests in
> Leon Co, Fla.
>
> Born on the plantation and wealthy. Enjoyed life
> as a cotton planter until the result of the civil
> war; despoiled of this wealth – attempted to
> adopt [sic] himself to the great changes on the
> plantation after the war – but his health giving
> way, had to turn affairs to his 18 yr old son.

169

Was an honorable, honest citizen. Respected by those he was known to. A Democrat, he voted as such; accepted no office though urged to enter politics. Avoided no debt of honor.

Called Major Ben, but held no war office. At one time being in Virginia, he shouldered his musket & tramped through the valley to repel a raid. Did not belong to the army, but with – musket was in the time of battle at Olustee, Fla – again at Newport and the Natural Bridge fights in Fla.

Was of the Methodist persuasion.

Being literary, gave much time to reading & was of fine information & splendid in conversation was very interesting at home and with friends.

TIMELINE

Benjamin Cadwallader Chaires (1847-1902), grandson of Benjamin Chaires

Plantation: Fauntleroy
Children: Alice Burroughs Chaires
            Ben C. Chaires IV
            Julia Pettus Chaires
            Mary Ann Chaires Hodges
            Octavia Chaires Price
            one unnamed orphan born in New Orleans from
            union with Martha Mash Chaires

1867   Ella Burroughs, future wife of Ben. C., born – Nov. 4

1876   Ben C. begins affair with Martha Mash Chaires –
       Feb. 18

1878   Charles Powell conveys title on land he purchased for
       Ben C and Octavia in 1870 to Ben C. and to Samuel
       Parkhill in trust for Octavia for $50.00. Land included
       1,200 acres, "constituting the plantation known as
       Fauntleroy." – Jan. 21

       Ben C. conveys to Henry Terrell Mash (Martha's
       brother) his 1/3 interest in the mill on CP's plantation,
       Ever May. The mill consists of a two story building that
       holds a cotton gin, screw and grist mill. All are powered
       by the same Burnhaud Turbine Water Wheel. – Feb. 18

       Ben C. named as the lover of his Uncle Charles's wife,
       Martha Mash, and is the father of her unborn child.
       Child was born in New Orleans in April and given to an
       asylum.

       New Orleans Capt. W.H. Manning finds 18 day old
       baby; parents unknown; sent to St. Vincent Infant
       Orphan Asylum – April 22

1879   Ben C. turns himself in for taking back mule from F.
       Hawkins – Jan. 16

       Charles and Ben C. shoot it out on Monroe St.; Ben C
       wounded in leg – Nov. 17

       Charles and Ben C. indicted for "carrying arms in
       secret" – Nov. 18

       Charles indicted for assault with intent to murder and
       jailed – Nov. 18

1880   Ben C. buys 1,878 acres from Charles Robert (son of
       Joseph) on Wakulla River in Wakulla Co. – Jan. 14

1882   Ben C. buys back Fauntleroy from Furman's widow,
        Mattie (sale to CP was in litigation for several years)

        Ben C. married Ella Ann Burroughs – probably 1882.

1883   Daughter Octavia born – Aug. 3

1885   Samuel Parkhill Chaires testifies that Ben C. lived at
        Fauntleroy during the affair w/ Martha (about a mile
        from Ever May)

1886   Daughter Mary Ann born – Oct. 6

1888   Mr. Benjamin C. Chaires, a successful and prosperous
        Leon County farmer, living four miles southeast of
        Tallahassee, the past season raised 2,000 bushels of
        corn, a large oat crop, killed seventy odd fat hogs and a
        large number of fine beef cattle. He raises his own
        horses and mules, has a large number of hogs and cows
        for another season, and has meat, corn, oats, etc. to sell.
        Mr. Chaires also has a fine orchard of choice varieties of
        peach trees and is putting out various kinds of grape
        vines, fruit trees, etc. – Feb. 23, *The Weekly Floridian*

1890   Daughter Julia Pettus born – March 1

1892   Daughter Alice Burroughs born – Dec. 16

1897   Ben C. serves as state legislator in the House (Leon
        County)

        Son Ben IV born – Nov. 16

1902   Ben C. dies – April 29

1915   Daughter Alice dies – Aug. 22

1921   Sister Octavia dies – May 13

1952   Wife Ella Burroughs dies – Dec. 14

1960   Daughter Mary Ann dies – April 3

1961   Son Benjamin IV dies – Dec. 21

1966   Daughter Octavia dies – January 20

1968   Daughter Julia Pettus dies – August 3

OBITUARY

The Weekly Tallahasseean
May 2, 1902

B.C. Chaires died at his country home 5 miles east of the city. At one time he was a member of the state legislature. He was about 55 years old. He leaves a wife, four daughters, one son and a sister.

Also in *The Weekly Tallahasseean*
May 2, 1902

B.C. CHAIRES DEAD

News reached Tallahassee early on Tuesday morning of the sudden death of Honorable B.C. Chaires, at his country home five miles east of the city. On Monday Mr. Chaires was apparently in as good health as he ever was, working in the field all day. He ate a hearty supper, but was shortly after seized with a violent pain in his left side. Home remedies were applied without avail. Mrs. Chaires wished to send for a physician, but her husband refused, thinking the attack would soon pass over.

He continued to grow worse, and about 1 o'clock Tuesday morning consented to have the physician sent for. Mr. Chaires

173

wrote the note himself, and a messenger was dispatched post haste. The sick man continued to grow rapidly worse, and passed away at 3 o'clock, before the doctor arrived. The cause of his death was acute indigestion.

Mr. Chaires was a prominent farmer of Leon county, highly respected by all who knew him. At one time he was a member of the State Legislature.

Deceased was about 55 years of age. He leaves a wife, four daughters and one son, also a sister, Mrs. Greenhow of this city.

Remains were interred in the Episcopal cemetery in this city at 5 o'clock Wednesday afternoon. The funeral cortege was met at the Houstoun place east of the city, by a number of Tallahassee friends, who escorted the body to its last resting place. Services were conducted at the grave by Reverend Dr. Carter, of the Episcopal church.

The funeral was under the direction of Undertaker Duncan. The pall-bearers were: Judge George P. Raney, T.H. Randolph, H.T. Felkel, R.J. Phillips, W.F. Quaile, and J.T. Jenkins.

EPITAPH

Benjamin C
Chaires
Born
May 14, 1847
Died
Apr 29, 1902
There was an angel
band in heaven
That was not quite
complete
So God took our
darling one
To fill the vacant seat

- Woodmen of the World

BURIAL

St. John's Episcopal Church Cemetery, Tallahassee.

*Benjamin C. Chaires is buried in his family's plot
with his wife and all of his children.*

Furman Chaires
(1823-1867)

Plantation: name unknown
Children: Louvinia (also spelled Lavinia) & Sally
             Josephine
             Thomas
             Mary
             Maria
             Lula

TIMELINE

1823   Furman born in St. Augustine – Oct. 20

1830   Mary Jones, future wife, born – Jan. 23

1845   Furman marries Mary E. Jones of Greenwood Plantation,
        Thomas County, GA – June 15

1846   Furman, Joseph and Green are appointed guardians of
        Thomas, Charles and Martha – May 25

1848   Buys portions of Sec. 20 & 21, T1R2, SE from John
        Alexander – July 10

1849   Lavinia and Sally born – May 2
        Sally dies – June 4, buried at Greenwood Plantation
        Cemetery, Thomasville, GA

1851   Josephine born – Jan. 5
        Buys E/2 of NE/4 of Sec. 20, T1R2, SE from John
        Shepherd – Dec. 3

1854   Thomas born – June 19, dies June 22, buried at Greenwood
        Plantation Cemetery, Thomasville, GA

177

Mary Jones dies – Sept. 22, buried at Greenwood
Plantation Cemetery, Thomasville, GA

1855   Furman designates Joseph to conduct his business while
        out of state – Sept.

1856   Furman enlists in Florida Mounted Volunteers – April-Oct.

        Furman a guest of Dr. J. A. Braden in Manatee County
        when attacked by Indians – April 1

1857   Josephine dies – Dec. 28, buried at Greenwood Plantation
        Cemetery, Thomasville, GA

1866   Ad in *Semi-Weekly Floridian* includes Furman in a
        company that manufactures Steam Engines in Jacksonville
        – March 20

        Announces that Mariano Papy will be his agent and
        attorney – April 13

1867   Furman dies – buried at St. John's Episcopal Church
        Cemetery, Tallahassee – Aug. 15

OBITUARY

Semi-Weekly Floridian
Friday, August 16, 1867

DEATH OF FURMAN CHAIRES.

We regret to announce the sudden death of this gentleman at his
residence in this city, late yesterday evening. He was an old citizen
and highly esteemed.

Furman's daughter, Maria, born between 1846 and 1848, is buried
at Verdura:

Her epitaph:

To
our little
MARIA
ET 9 Mo. 11 Days
of such is the Kingdom of Heaven

Sarah Jane Chaires Ward
(1825-1859)

Plantation: Southwood
Children: George R.
           William
           Annie
           Sallie C. or Butler
           Mattie
           Mary

1810   future husband George T. Ward born – Jan. 8

1825   Sarah born in Jacksonville – December 12

1844   George and Sarah enter into a pre-marital agreement – Feb. 7
        (Sarah may use her property – left to her by her father –
        independently of George and she will not be liable for any of
        his debts. The land is "in trust" for her, overseen by George,
        but she has final say in how it is used or disposed of.)

        Marries George T. Ward at Verdura – Feb. 8

1856   Ward takes out a loan from the Union Bank to buy 1,280
        acres that becomes Southwood. The loan includes payment
        for 61 slaves that had belonged to Hector Braden but were
        released to Ward as part of the agreement – March 19

1859   Sarah dies in Bibb County (possibly Macon) GA –
        October 31

181

The Georgia *Journal & Messenger*
November 9, 1859

DEATH OF MRS. WARD

We regret to announce that Mrs. Ward, wife of our old and esteemed friend, Major George T. Ward, of Florida, died in this city on the 30ᵗʰ ultimo. She was the daughter of the late Major Ben Chaires, of Florida. Her sickness was of a protracted character. Her bereaved companion and friends have our sincere condolence. The remains of Mrs. Ward were taken to Florida.

EPITAPH

SACRED
TO THE MEMORY OF
SARAH JANE CHAIRES
WIFE OF
GEORGE T. WARD
BORN DECEMBER 12, 1825
DIED OCTOBER 31, 1859

"BLESSED ARE THE DEAD WHO DIE IN THE LORD."

BURIAL

Southwood (behind the main house)

TIMELINE

George T. Ward (1810-1862), husband of Sarah Jane Chaires

1862   George T. Ward (officer in 2nd Florida Infantry) dies at Battle of Williamsburg – May 5

1874   Southwood is put up for public sale – after the 1st Monday in November.

BURIAL

Bruton Parish Episcopal Church Cemetery, Williamsburg, Virginia

Thomas Butler Chaires
(1828-1880)

Plantations: Tiger Tail
            Verdura
Children: Josephine (Fenie)
            Gabriella (Ella)
            Sallie Powell
            Mattie Osee Lillian
            Mary Salter
            Fannie

1828   Thomas Butler born in Leon County – July 21
(Probably named for Thomas Fitch's administrator,
Thomas Butler in East Florida, who arranged the
transaction between Ben Chaires and Thomas Fitch to
purchase the 4,500 acres on Halifax River; eventually
this area is known as Holly Hill, FL.) Chaires also held
200 acres in common with Thomas Butler on the Plains
and Swamps of San Diego. Also, a family story indicates
that Ben Chaires called the highest point at Verdura
"Butler Hill.") – 1834

Future wife Sarah (Sally) Salter was born in KY –
April 17

1850   Thomas and Charles joint heads of household on census

1854   Thomas advertises in Augusta, Marianna and Albany
papers to sell an engine and various parts for a grist mill
– April 15

Thomas marries Sally Salter – Sept. 19

1855   Josephine born – Nov. 29

185

1856   Thomas serves as juror in Leon County Circuit Court

1857   Fannie born – Sept. 26

1858   Heirs sell their shares of Verdura to Charles and Thomas
        – May 18

        Fannie dies – June 21

1859   Ben Jr. sells a lot of land in T1R1, SE and slaves to TB.
        TB then makes Ben Jr. trustee of Octavia and Ben C. (to
        prevent Ben Jr. having to sell land to pay "alimony" to
        Mary Shepherd)

        Gabriella born – May 9

1861   Charles, Thomas, Green D on Levy County tax rolls

        Sallie Powell born – May 22

1862   TB and CP buy land in Levy County (T13S, R13E) –
        Nov. 14

        Mary Salter born – Oct. 31

1865   Thomas petitions for amnesty and pardon – June 28

        Charles and Thomas lease plantation to cousin Green A.
        for $5,000 in gold plus profits from crops and livestock
        for one year – Nov. 16

        Charles and Thomas lease Verdura to William K. Beard
        and Robert Gamble Shepard for $2,500 in gold –

        Nov. 18

1867   Charles and Thomas bring suit against William K. Beard
        and Robert G. Shepard for non-payment of Verdura
        lease; asks $5,000 in back payment and damages –
        March

Charles and Thomas individually bring suit against cousin Green A. for non-payment of lease and damage to equipment; ask $10,000 in back payment and damages (evidently leased Tiger Tail and Ever May individually) – March

1870   Charles and Thomas on Levy County census in Cedar Keys (Atsena Otie)

1872   Chaires and Co (partnership dissolved prior to Jan. 1, 1872) sue Robert Raines for non-payment of tobacco purchased in 1866

Mattie Osee Lillian born – June 5

1874   Charles and Thomas secure a loan from Earle and Perkins with mortgage on Verdura (except the 3 acres including the graveyard and the Burgess Tract) – March 28

1877   Thomas and Sallie Salter deed their share of Verdura to Charles – Dec. 3

Mary Salter dies – April 18

1878   Thomas sells his interest in Verdura to Charles so that he can pay off the loan to Earle and Perkins; Charles gives Thomas an interest in the Mill at Ever May – Feb.

1879   TB and Sallie lease Tiger Tail to Robert and James Monroe to pay off debts. For their own use, they retain dwelling house, smokehouse, kitchen, stable, garden and 160 acres contiguous to the house.

1880   Thomas Butler dies intestate – July 20; said to be buried at Verdura "at the time of his death he was possessed of a large and valuable estate consisting of both real and personal property."

1884   Sallie petitions the court that she be made administrator of TB's estate. She asks that the Notary in Cedar Keys be allowed to administer oaths as she is living too far away from Tallahassee – presumably at Cedar Keys. It was so decreed. A bond of $6,000.00 was set. – Feb. 18

1892   Sallie dies – May 22; she is the last family member thought to be buried at Verdura.

No obituary, epitaph or grave marker found for Thomas Butler

No obituary, epitaph or grave marker found for Sallie Salter

Note: Many descendants of Thomas Butler Chaires are citizens of Levy County today.

Martha A. Chaires
(1827-1866)

Plantations: Bolton
      Welaunee
Children: Robert Grattan
      Howard
      Jennie (Sarah Jane)
      Lettie (Letitia)

1815   Future husband Robert Howard Gamble born in Bottetourt County, Virginia

1829   Martha A. born in Leon County, FL

1850   Martha has 56 slaves on census

1852   Land in 1N, 2E deeded to Martha – Sept. 1

1858   Martha marries Robert Howard Gamble – June 7

     Martha conveys her plantation, Bolton, to Green and George T. Ward, in trust, to protect her property, her share of her father's lands in East Florida, and her 68 slaves – June 8

1860   Nephew Benjamin Burgess dies at age 28 at her home; leaves his estate to his father and Aunt Martha – July 6; buried at Verdura

1864   Gamble serves as Captain of Gamble's Artillery during the Battle of Olustee – Feb.

1866   Martha dies – Jan. 24 or 27 (?), buried at St. John's Episcopal Church Cemetery

OBITUARY

Tallahassee *Semi-Weekly Floridian*
January 30, 1866

DIED in this city, on Thursday, the 24th ult., Mrs. MARTHA C. GAMBLE, wife of Col. Robert H. Gamble, aged thirty-nine years.

It is seldom permitted to friendship to record the departure of a lady whose virtues and graces secured the esteem of those with whom she associated in a more eminent degree. In early life she displayed those qualities which, as time advanced, were matured into a character at once dignified, elevated and refined and illustrated by an intelligence which made her society agreeable and attractive to all who made her acquaintance. In the hospitable home of her husband she was indeed as she appeared, the presiding spirit which harmonized the intercourse of all, both old and young, and dispensed the courtesies and charities of social life with an open and unselfish hand.

But the most beautiful exhibition of her character is to be found in the devotion she displayed to those to whom she was bound by the ties of kindred, and especially when circumstances placed them under her supervision and guidance. No sacrifice of personal comfort was too great – no care nor trouble too much to be submitted to by her to promote their comfort, increase their gifts, or secure their welfare.

To her immediate family – husband and children – she was all that affection could ask or duty demand. These at last are the graces that endear us to our kind, and they were the adornments that illustrated her life.

Her last moments were no unfit termination of her previous existence, for peacefully did she descend to the tomb, leaving her sorrowing friends not "without hope" that "our loss is her gain," and that she now reposes in final rest from the cares and sorrows that attend us in this life.

Note: The date of Martha's death is in question. The obituary indicates that she died in the preceding month of December, but the 24th was not on a Thursday that year. The 24th of January was not on a Thursday either – so the date is incorrect or the day of the week is incorrect. Her year of birth is also uncertain. The obituary would have her age 39 at the time of death which would place her birth year at 1827. Her gravestone birth year is 1829.

EPITAPH

MARTHA A. CHAIRES
wife of
ROBERT HOWARD GAMBLE
1829 - 1866
He giveth his beloved sleep

BURIAL

St. John's Episcopal Church Cemetery

Charles Powell Chaires
(1830-1881)

Plantations: Ever May
                Verdura
Children: None

Please see Chapter 8 for a description of the events in Charles's life that are specifically related to Verdura and his relationships with other members of the Benjamin Chaires family.

OBITUARY

Land of Flowers
October 1881

Mr. Charles Powell Chaires, an old resident of this county, died at the St. Marks lighthouse on the 26th of July.

Note: His actual date of death was August 17, 1881.

No epitaph or grave marker was found for Charles Powell Chaires.

Josephine Chaires
(1832 – 1840)

Died in childhood

<u>EPITAPH</u>

JOSEPHINE
DAUGHTER OF
BENJAMIN AND SARAH CHAIRS [*sic*]
DIED OCTOBER 21st, 1840
AGED 8 YEARS &
6 MONTHS

Of such is the Kingdom of Heaven

<u>BURIAL</u>

Verdura Plantation

Martha Mash Chaires Thomas
(1842 – 1911)

Please see Chapter 8 for details regarding Martha's life as the estranged wife of Charles Powell Chaires.

Children:
One child was born of her union with Benjamin Cadwallader Chaires ("Ben C."). The child was left in an orphanage asylum in New Orleans shortly after its birth.

OBITUARY

The Thomasville *Enterprise*
November 2, 1911

FUNERAL TOMORROW MORNING

Services Over the Remains of Mrs.
Frank Thomas at the Residence
At Nine Thirty O'Clock

Mrs. Frank Thomas died at her home in the East End this morning at ten minutes of ten, after an illness of about ten days with fever. The end came peacefully to this beloved woman in the presence of her loved ones. The funeral Services will be held tomorrow morning at 9:30, at the residence. Rev. Robert Harris, of Cairo, officiating. Interment at Beachton at 1:30.

Mrs. Thomas is survived by her husband and sister and brothers Mrs. Reddin Smith, M. M. Mash, J.J. Mash and H.T. Mash. The friends of these families are invited to be present at the funeral tomorrow morning.

The death of Mrs. Thomas will cause deep regret in Thomasville and Thomas county [*sic*], where she lived for many years and made hundreds of friends.

<u>EPITAPH</u>

Martha Chaires Thomas
Feb. 18, 1842
Nov. 2, 1911

<u>BURIAL</u>

Ochlocknee Baptist Church in Beachton, Georgia. (Beachton was formerly known as Duncanville.)

Bibliography/References

Books, Articles, Reports, Compilations

Adams, William Hampton, and Sarah Jane Boling. "Status and Ceramics for Planters and Slaves on Three Georgia Coastal Plantations." In *Approaches to Material Culture Research for Historical Archaeologists*, compiled by George L. Miller, Olive R. Jones, Lester A. Ross and Teresita Majewski. California, PA: The Society for Historical Archaeology, 1991.

Adams, William R., and Paul L. Weaver III. *Historic Places of St. Augustine and St. Johns County: A Visitor's Guide*. St. Augustine, FL: Southern Heritage Press, 1993.

Alden and Associates, Compilers. *Jefferson and Burke County, Georgia Early Records*. Albany, GA: Alden and Associates, 1965.

Baptist, Edward E. *Creating an Old South: Middle Florida's Plantation Frontier before the Civil War*. Chapel Hill: University of North Carolina Press, 2002.

Barrow, Lee G. *Early Court Records of Pulaski County, Georgia 1809-1825*. Greenville, SC: Southern Historical Press, 1994.

Blake, Sallie E. *Tallahassee of Yesterday*. Tallahassee, FL: T. J. Appleyard, 1924.

Blair, Reeves F. *Historic American Building Survey (HABS): "The Columns," Benjamin Chaires House*. Philadelphia: National Park Service, 1962.

Blair, Ruth, ed. *Some Early Tax Digests of Georgia*. N.p.: Georgia Department of Archives and History, 1926.

Blassingame, John W. *The Slave Community: Plantation Life in the Antebellum South.* New York: Oxford University Press, 1972.

Bouknecht, Carol Cox, Compiler. *Florida Juror and Witness Certificates, Leon County, 1847-1862, 1876-1879, 1885.* Tallahassee, FL: Carol Cox Bouknecht, 1991.

Boyd, Mark F. "The Apalachicola or Chattahoochee Arsenal of the United States." *Apalachee* 4 (1950-1956).

Brown, Cantor."The Florida Crisis of 1826-27 and the Second Seminole War." *The Florida Historical Quarterly* 73, no. 4 (1995).

————. *Ossian Bingley Hart: Florida's Loyalist Reconstruction Governor.* Baton Rouge: Louisiana State University Press, 1997.

Brueckheimer, William R. *Leon County Hunting Plantations: An Historical and Architectural Survey, Final Report: Geographical-Historical Overview, Volume 1.* Tallahassee: Florida Department of State, Historic Tallahassee Preservation Board, 1988.

Brueckheimer, William R., Sara Hay Lamb, and Gwendolyn B. Waldorf. *Rural Resources of Leon County, Florida, 1821-1950, Volume 1: Historic Contexts and Case Studies.* Tallahassee: Florida Department of State, Historic Tallahassee Preservation Board, 1992.

Carter, Clarence Edwin, Compiler and Editor. *Territorial Papers of the United States, Volume XXII: The Territory of Florida, 1821-1824.* Washington, DC: United States Government Printing Office, 1956.

————. *Territorial Papers of the United States, Volume XXIV: The Territory of Florida, 1828-1834*. Washington, DC: United States Government Printing Office, 1959.

"Claims to East Florida Lands by Arredondo, Report Number 9." *American State Papers* 5.

"Claims to East Florida Lands by Chaires, Report Numbers 1, 8, 74, 47." *American State Papers* 5.

Clinton, Catherine. *The Plantation Mistress*. New York: Pantheon Books, 1982.

"The Chaires Family." In *Pioneer Florida: Personal and Family Records*. Tampa: Southern Publishing, 1959.

Coles, David J. "The Florida Diaries of Daniel H. Wiggins, 1836-1841." *The Florida Historical Quarterly* 73, no. 4 (1995).

Crumpton, Daniel Nathan, Compiler. *Jefferson County, Georgia Land Records*. Warrenton, GA: Daniel Nathan Crumpton, 2003.

Cusick, James G. *The Other War of 1812: The Patriot War and the American Invasion of Spanish East Florida*. Athens: University of Georgia Press, 2007.

Davidson, Alvie, Compiler. *Florida Land: Records of the Tallahassee and Newnansville General Land Office, 1825-1892*. Westminster, MD: Heritage Books, 2008.

Davis, Mary Lamar. *The Columns*. Tallahassee, FL: Leon County Public Library, 1958.

Davis, Thomas Frederick. *History of Jacksonville, Florida and Vicinity*. Jacksonville: Florida Historical Society, 1925.

————. *History of Early Jacksonville, Florida: Being an Authentic Record of Events from the Earliest Times to and including the Civil War*. Jacksonville, FL: Jacksonville Board of Trade, 1911.

Denham, James M. *Florida Founder William P. DuVal, Frontier Bon Vivant*. Columbia: University of South Carolina Press, 2015.

Denny, Philippa, and Tommie A. Wasden. *A Look at Louisville: Photos from Our Past*. Louisville: Louisville GA Bicentennial Commemoration, 1986.

Dickerson, Joseph A., Compiler. "Descendants of Benjamin Chaires." In *The Cheairs Index*. Chattanooga: N. H. Cheairs, 1991, updated 2000.

Dodd, Dorothy. "The Tallahassee Railroad and the Town of St. Marks." *Apalachee* 4 (1950-1956).

Doran, Glen H., and Rochelle A. Marrinan. *Rural Resources of Leon County, Florida, 1821-1950, Volume 2: An Archaeological Investigation of the Charles Bannerman Plantation and Theus-Roberts Farm*. Tallahassee: Florida Department of State, Historic Tallahassee Preservation Board, 1992.

Dovell, J.E., and J.G. Richardson. *History of Banking in Florida, 1828-1954*. Orlando: Florida Bankers Association, 1955.

Ellis, Mary, and William Warren Rogers. *Tallahassee and Leon County: A History and Bibliography*. Tallahassee: Florida Department of State, 1986.

Eppes, Susan Bradford. *The Negro of the Old South: A Bit of Period History*. Chicago: Joseph G. Branch, 1925.

———. *Through Some Eventful Years*. Facsimile of the 1926 edition, with an introduction and index by Joseph D. Cushman Jr. Gainesville: University of Florida Press, 1968.

Evans, Tad, Compiler. *Early Court Records of Pulaski County, Georgia 1809-1825*. Greenville, SC: Southern Historical Press, 1998.

———. *Georgia Newspaper Clippings, Laurens County Extracts, 1810-1892*. Savannah, GA: Tad Evans, 1998.

———. *Thomas County Newspaper Clippings (1857-1875)*. Savannah, GA: T. Evans, 1995.

———. *Thomas County Newspaper Clippings (1882-1888)*. Savannah, GA: T. Evans, 1996.

Fairbanks, Charles. "The Kingsley Slave Cabins in Duval County, Florida, 1968." *Conference on Historic Site Archaeology Papers* 7 (1974).

Fletcher, Daniel. "Once Proud Chaires Mansion Now Lies in Ruins." *Southern Historical News* 19, no. 22 (1999).

Florida State Library Board. *Transcriptions of Public Archives in Florida, Ordinances of the City of St. Augustine 1821-1827, Volume 1*. Jacksonville: Florida Historical Records Survey, 1941.

Forbes, James Grant. *Sketches, Historical and Topographical of The Floridas*. New York: C.S. Van Winkle, 1821.

Gannon, Michael. *Florida: A Short History*. Gainesville: University Press of Florida, 1993.

Giddings, Joshua Reed. *The Exiles of Florida: Or, the Crimes Committed by Our Government against the Maroons Who Fled from South Carolina and Other Slave States, Seeking*

Protection under Spanish Laws. Columbus, OH: Follett, Foster, 1858.

Gresham, Carling. *Territorial Florida Banks and Bonds, 1821-1845*. N.p.: C. Gresham, 1993.

Groene, Bertram H. *Ante-Bellum Tallahassee*. Tallahassee: Florida Heritage Foundation, 1981.

Gunnell, S. E. *Search for Yesterday: A History of Levy County, Florida*. Bronson, FL: Levy County Archives Committee, 1976.

Hadd, Donald. "The Columns, 1830-1860." *Apalachee* 5 (1957-1962).

Hartz, Fred R., and Emilie K. Hartz, Compilers. *Genealogical Abstracts from the Georgia Journal (Milledgeville) Newspaper, Volume I (1809-1818)*. Vidalia, GA: Gwendolyn Press, 1990.

―――. *Genealogical Abstracts from the Georgia Journal (Milledgeville) Newspaper, Volume II (1819-1823)*. Vidalia, GA: Gwendolyn Press, 1992.

―――. *Genealogical Abstracts from the Georgia Journal (Milledgeville) Newspaper, Volume III (1824-1828)*. Vidalia, GA: Gwendolyn Press, 1994.

Heiland, Sharyn. "Report on North Structure Excavation (8Le1211)." Unpublished manuscript in the *Florida Master Site File (Manuscript #19210)*. Tallahassee: Florida Department of State, Division of Historical Resources, Bureau of Historic Preservation, 2010.

―――. "Report on Verdura Graveyard Clean-up Day (8Le4192)." Unpublished manuscript in the *Florida Master Site File (Manuscript #22409)*. Tallahassee: Florida

Department of State, Division of Historical Resources, Bureau of Historic Preservation, 2007.

———. "A Scandal in Old Tallahassee." *Tallahassee Magazine,* November-December 2004.

———. "The Verdura Place: A Historical Overview and Preliminary Archaeological Survey." Master's thesis, Florida State University, 2001.

Heuman, Gad J., and James Walvin, eds. *The Slavery Reader.* Volume 1 of *Routledge Readers in History.* London: Routledge, 2003.

Hughes, Nathaniel Cheairs, Jr. *The Cheairs Index.* Chattanooga, TN: N.C. Hughes, 1991.

Index to U. S. Census of Georgia, 1820. Baltimore: Genealogical Publishing, 1969.

Institute of Historic Research. *1830 Private Land Claims in East Florida.* Signal Mountain, TN: Institute of Historic Research, [199-?].

Joyner, Charles. "The World of the Plantation Slaves." In *Before Freedom Came: African-American Life in the Antebellum South,* edited by Edward D. C. Campbell, Jr. and Kym S. Rice. Charlottesville: University Press of Virginia, 1991.

Kane, Sharyn, and Richard Keaton. *Beneath These Waters: Archeological and Historical Studies of 11,500 Years Along the Savannah River.* Atlanta: Interagency Archeological Services Division, National Park Service, Southeast Region, 1993.

Kenneson, Claude, Compiler. *Extracts from Accounts of Travelers, Visitors, Journalists and Others to Tallahassee, Florida: 1825-1925.* N.p.: n.p., n.d.

Keuchel, Edward F., and Joe Knetsch. "Settlers, Bureaucrats and Private Land Claims." *The Florida Historical Quarterly* 63, no. 2 (October 1989).

Knetsch, Joe. *Spanish Land Grants: A Problem for Florida Surveyors: The Case of George J. F. Clarke.* Tallahassee: Florida Department of Environmental Protection, Division of State Lands, 2008.

Knowles, Joshua. *Methodism in Tallahassee in the Year 1836.* Tallahassee: n.p., 1878.

Landry, Hazel, and Eliza Landry. "The Chaires Family of Leon County." *Magnolia Monthly* 6 (1968).

———. "The Chaires Family of Leon County and Their In-Laws." *Magnolia Monthly* 6 (1968).

Lane, Pedie. "The Spirit of Cedar Key." *Florida Living*, 1999.

Mahon, John K. "The Treaty of Moultrie Creek, 1823." *The Florida Historical Quarterly* 40, no. 4 (1962).

Manley, Walter W., E. Cantor Brown, and Eric W. Rise, eds. *The Supreme Court of Florida and Its Predecessor Courts, 1821-1917.* Gainesville: University Press of Florida, 1997.

McGuire, Randall H., and Robert Paynter, eds. *The Archaeology of Inequality.* Cambridge, MA: Basil Blackwell, 1991.

Mills, Donna Rachel. *Florida's Unfortunates: The 1880 Federal Census: Defective, Dependent, and Delinquent Classes.* Tuscaloosa: Mills Historical Press, 1993.

The Narrative of Amos Dresser, with Stone's Letters from Natchez: An Obituary Notice of the Writer, and Two Letters from Tallahassee, Relating to the Treatment of Slaves. New York: American Anti-Slavery Society, 1836.

Orser, Charles E. *The Material Basis of the Postbellum Tenant Plantation*. Athens: University of Georgia Press, 1988.

Orser, Charles E., Annette M. Nekolai, and James L. Roark. *Exploring the Rustic Life: Multidisciplinary Research at Millwood Plantation, a Large Piedmont Plantation in Abbeville County, South Carolina and Elbert County, Georgia*. Chicago: Mid-American Research Center, Loyola University, 1987.

Paisley, Clifton. *From Cotton to Quail: An Agricultural Chronicle of Leon County, Florida, 1860-1968*. Gainesville: University of Florida Press, 1968.

————. *The Red Hills of Florida, 1528-1865*. Tuscaloosa: University of Alabama Press, 1989.

Paisley, Joy Smith. *The Cemeteries of Leon County, Florida: Rural, White Cemeteries: Tombstone Inscriptions and Epitaphs*. Tallahassee, FL: Colonial Dames XVII Century, 1977.

Parker, Daisy. "The Leon County Court, 1825-1833." *Apalachee* 3 (1948-1950).

Phelps, John B. *People of Lawmaking in Florida, 1822-1995*. Tallahassee: Florida House of Representatives, 1995.

Phillips, Ulrich B., and James D. Glunt, eds. *Florida Plantation Records*. St. Louis: Missouri Historical Society, 1927.

Rivers, Larry Eugene. *Slavery in Florida: Territorial Days to Emancipation*. Gainesville: University Press of Florida, 2000.

Rogers, William W. *Antebellum Thomas County 1825-1861*. Tallahassee: Florida State University Press, 1963.

Rogers, William W., and Erica R. Clark. *The Croom Family and Goodwood Plantation: Land, Litigation and Southern Lives.* Athens: University of Georgia Press, 1999.

Schafer, Daniel L. *Zephaniah Kingsley Jr. and the Atlantic World: Slave Trader, Plantation Owner, Emancipator.* Gainesville: University Press of Florida, 2013.

Schweikart, Larry. *Banking in the American South from the Age of Jackson to Reconstruction.* Baton Rouge: Louisiana State University Press, 1987.

Shofner, Jerrell H. *Nor Is It Over Yet: Florida in the Era of Reconstruction, 1863-1877.* Gainesville: University Presses of Florida, Gainesville, 1974.

Singleton, Theresa A. *The Archaeology of Slavery and Plantation Life.* Orlando: Academic Press, 1985.

Smith, Elizabeth. "Robert Gamble of Welaunee Plantation II." *Magnolia Monthly* 10 (1972).

Snodgrass, Dena. *Dee-Dot Ranch and Twenty Mile House: A History.* Jacksonville, FL: Jacksonville Historical Society, 1973.

Stampp, Kenneth M. *The Peculiar Institution: Slavery in the Ante-bellum South.* New York: Vintage Books, 1956.

"St. Joseph, An Episode of the Economic and Political History of Florida." *The Florida Historical Quarterly* 5, no. 4 (1927).

"Table of Florida Counties in 1836." In *The History of Jackson County, Florida.* N.p.: Jackson County Historical Society, 1950.

Thomas, Allen, Compiler and Editor. *Laurens County Georgia Legal Records, 1807-1832*. Roswell, GA: W.H. Wolfe Associates, 1991.

Thompson, Shirley Joiner. *The People of East Florida during the Revolutionary War—War of 1812 Period*. Kingsland, GA: Shirley Joiner Thompson, 1982.

Turner, Gregg. *A Short History of Florida Railroads*. Charleston, SC: Arcadia Publishing, 2003.

Varick, Floreda, and Phyllis Rose Smith. *Thomas County, Georgia, 1850 Census*. Cairo, GA: n.p., 1978.

Vickrey, Duke, Compiler. *Dates for Patent Certificates on Land Grants, Federal Land Grants, First Purchaser* (Leon County Reconstructed Tract Book). Gulf Breeze, FL: Duke Vickrey, 1998.

———. Index to *Reconstructed Federal Land Tracts (Jackson County)*. Gulf Breeze, FL: Duke Vickrey, 1998.

Vlach, John Michael. *Back of the Big House: The Architecture of Plantation Slavery*. Chapel Hill: University of North Carolina Press, 1993.

Warner, Lee H. *Free Men in an Age of Servitude: Three Generations of a Black Family*. Lexington: University Press of Kentucky, 1992.

Wiedenfield, M. "Architectural Survey of the Historic Sites of Thomasville Road. State Survey #3150." Manuscript in *Florida Master Site File*. Tallahassee: Florida Department of State, Division of Historical Resources, Bureau of Historic Preservation, 1986.

Williams, John Lee. *The Territory of Florida: Or, Sketches of the Topography, Civil and Natural History, of the Country, the Climate, and the Indian Tribes, from the First Discovery to the Present Time.* New York: A.T. Goodrich, 1837.

Wilson, Emily L., Compiler. *Abstracts from Superior and Circuit Court Case Files, St. Johns County, Volume II.* Jacksonville: Florida Historical Records Survey, 1939.

Ziewitz, Kathryn, and June Wiaz. *Green Empire: The St. Joe Company and the Remaking of Florida's Panhandle.* Gainesville: University Press of Florida, 2004.

On File at the State Archives of Florida

Acts and Resolutions of the General Assembly of the State of Florida, Passed at Its Eighth Session, Published by Authority of Law under the Direction of the Attorney General, Tallahassee, 1857.

Arredondo and Son, 289,645 Acres Center of Which is in Micanopy, December 22, 1817. Spanish Land Grants.

Arredondo, J.M., 20,000 Acres at Big Hammock, Alachua, March 20, 1817. Spanish Land Grants.

Chaires, Benjamin. Benjamin Chaires v Zephaniah Kingsley and Philip R. Yonge, 1831. Territorial Court of Appeals Case Files 1825-1846. S 73.

———. Central Bank v Bank of Magnolia, 1834. Territorial Court of Appeals Case Files 1825-1846. S 73.

———. Letter of Agreement on Purchase of Slaves, May 10, 1820.

———. Letter to Thomas Fitch in St. Marys, GA, May 27, 1820.

————. Will, 1835. Index to Estates, Book 1, No. 31, Leon County Courthouse.

Chaires, Benjamin, Paul Dupon, C.W. Denton, and Thomas Fitch. Memorandum of Agreement, July 22, 1818.

Chaires, Benjamin, Thomas Fitch, and James Taylor. Agreement for Each to Pay $1,000 on Amelia Island Purchase, 1818.

Chaires, Charles Powell. Will, 1879. Leon County Will Book B.

Chaires, Green A. Contract for Hiring of Persons, 1860.

Chaires, Green D. Will, 1882. Leon County Probate File #916.

Chaires, Joseph. Letter Offering to Pay for Services of Surveyor, July 28, 1843. Miscellaneous Letters to the Surveyor General 1, 1825-1848.

————. Letter Requesting a New Survey, June 6, 1843. Miscellaneous Letters to the Surveyor General 1, 1825-1848.

Chaires, Martha Mash. Letter from Dresden, TN, July 23, 1878.

————. Letter from Dresden, TN, June 16, 1878.

————. Letter from New Orleans, LA, April 15, 1878.

Deed of Sale for 600 Acres and 57 Slaves on Amelia Island, Conveyed in Savannah, May 26, 1818. Thomas Fitch Letters.

Agricultural Census. Leon County, Florida. 1850, 1860, 1870, 1880.

Federal Census. Leon County, Florida. 1830, 1840, 1850, 1860, 1870, 1880.

————. Leon County, Florida. Slave Schedules. 1850, 1860.

Florida Department of Transportation. Aerial Photograph of Leon County, Township 1 South, Range 2 East, 1965, 1973, 1987, 1996.

Henderson, John A. Petition to the 2nd Judicial Circuit of Leon County for Permission to Sell Lands from Chaires's Estate, 1874.

Leon County. Chancery Court Record Numbers 50, 279, 297, 307, 319, 925, and 932.

————. Circuit Court Case Numbers 58, 653, 6530, 6578, 6645, 6777, and 7049.

————. Circuit Court Minutes, Book 8.

————. Deed Record Numbers A40, A172, B577, C243, C585, C612, C619, C643, D26, D51, D520, E581, F47, E771, G145, I142, L648, M70, M341, M669, O172, P372, R190, R112, R417, U218, U326, U345, U346, U448, U460, W237, CC175, CC249, FF456, and II545.

————. Inventory and Appraisements, Book D.

————. Mortgage Record Numbers E36, P377, R427-429, U322, X237, and X456.

————. Notice of Commissioners' Sale. May 27, 1842.

————. Orders at Chambers, Book A.

————. Probate File Numbers 31, 89, 373, 428A, 704, and 853.

————. State of Florida Census, 1885.

————. State of Florida Mortality Schedule, 1885.

————. Tax Records: Benjamin Chaires, 1829, 1839, and 1843-1848; Black Taxpayers, 1873-1880; Charles Powell and

Thomas Butler Chaires, 1850-1855, 1863, 1868, and 1873-1877; Charles Powell Chaires, 1851-1863, 1866-1868, and 1873-1878; Charles Powell Chaires Estate, 1880-1894; Sarah Powell Chaires, 1844-1848; Thomas Butler Chaires, 1851-1863, 1866-1868, and 1873-1877.

―――. Territorial Census, 1825.

Levy County. Conveyance of Acreage to Charles Powell and Thomas Butler, November 14, 1862. Register of Public Lands for the State of Florida.

―――. Tax Records: 1861-1879.

McGinniss, B.A., County Judge. Recording of Benjamin Chaires's Will, 1911. Will Book B.

Minutes. Board Meeting, Leon County Schools, December 1, 1881.

Nassau County. Deed Record, Book P, Page 81.

Powell, Jeremiah. Benjamin Chaires v John H. McIntosh, 1835. Territorial Court of Appeals Case Files 1825-1846. S 73.

―――. A Journal of Proceedings of the Legislative Council of the Territory of Florida at Its Fourteenth Session, Tallahassee, 1836.

St. Augustine City Council. Minute Book, 1821-1823.

St. Johns County. Deed Record Numbers H246, G69, H203, H204, L97, B145, B142, G177, G176, H367, H365, H251, H202, H249, H248, I-J109, and I-J88.

―――. Inventory of Miscellaneous File of Court Papers, Volume 1, A-O.

Walker, Samuel, Leon County Judge. Petition by Chaires's Heirs for Appointment of John A. Henderson as Administrator, 1873.

Wiggins, Daniel. Personal Diary, 1839-40.

Georgia Public Records

Baldwin County and Wilkinson County. Land Lottery, 1805. Mary Washington Museum, Macon.

Baldwin County Marriages, Book A, 1806-1836. County Probate Office, Milledgeville.

Burkes County Legal Records. William G. Jones to Benjamin Chaires, September 13, 1823. Mary Washington Museum, Macon.

Georgia Tax Digest. Jefferson County, 1796, 1799, 1816, 1820, 1822, 1824. Mary Washington Museum, Macon.

Jefferson County. Court Records. Court of Ordinary Minutes, 1801-1815. Mary Washington Museum, Macon.

Laurens County Court of Ordinary. Administrators and Guardian Bonds, Book A, 1809-1823. Laurens County Library, Dublin.

Laurens County. Estate Records, Inventories and Appraisements, Book A, 1808-1823. Mary Washington Museum, Macon.

Laurens County Marriages (Dublin), Volume 1, A-K, 1807-1892. Laurens County Library, Dublin.

Laurens County Superior Court. Deeds and Mortgages, 1801-1810. Laurens County Library, Dublin.

214

—. Deeds and Mortgages, Book E, 1815-1818. Laurens County Library, Dublin.

—. Deeds and Mortgages, Book I, 1826-1831. Laurens County Library, Dublin.

Pulaski County. Deed Books A, B, C, D, 1807-1816. Mary Washington Museum, Macon.

Thomas County. Georgia Records, Book E. Thomas County Courthouse, Thomasville.

U.S. Government Documents

United States Congress. *American State Papers, Documents of the Congress of the United States in Relation to the Public Lands*. Washington, DC: Gales and Seaton, 1860.

—. Journal of the House of Representatives of the United States. 18th Cong., 1st sess., May 20, 1924.

—. Journal of the Senate, Congressional Edition. February 9, 1846.

"Memorial of the Inhabitants' of East Florida District Petition for Tax Relief, November 25, 1822." In *Territorial Papers of the United States for the Territory of Florida, 1821-1845*. National Archives Microfilm Publication 721.

United States v. Arredondo. 31 U.S. 6 Pet. 591 (1832).

United States v. Benjamin Chaires and Others. 35 U.S. 308 (1836).

Transcript of the Record of the Superior Court of the District of East Florida in the Case of Joseph Chaires, Executor of Benjamin Chaires, Deceased, Peter Miranda and Gad

Humphreys vs. The United States of America Petition to Reform the Decree of said Court in a certain Land Claim On Appeal to the Supreme Court of the United States, No. 131, 1844. Record Group 267, Appellate Case File Number 2426. National Archives, Washington.

Florida Newspaper Articles and Advertisements

Chaires, Ben. "Withdrawal from Constitutional Convention." *Floridian and Advocate* (Tallahassee), September 25, 1838.

Chaires, Ben Jr. "Plantation for Sale." *Floridian and Journal* (Tallahassee), January 3, 1882.

Chaires, Joseph. "Notice." *Floridian and Advocate*, October 13, 1838.

———. "Notice." *Floridian and Advocate* (Tallahassee), January 12, 1839.

———. "Notice." *Herald and Southern Democrat* (St. Augustine), May 30, August 29, August 15, July 18, May 9, June 6, October 25, September 5, June 13, and June 20, 1839.

Chaires, Samuel P., and John A. Henderson. "Executors' Sale." *Weekly Floridian* (Tallahassee), January 3, 1882.

Chaires, Thomas Butler, and Charles Powell. "Valuable Plantation for Sale." Advertisement in *Floridian and Journal* (Tallahassee), October 2, 1858.

DeFord, Susan. "Family Planted Seeds of Tradition in Chaires." *Democrat* (Tallahassee), January 25, 1982.

Democrat (Tallahassee). "Grand Mansion in Ruins." March 28, 1974.

———. "Interview with Alice Burroughs Chaires." June 9, 1963.

———. "'Tay' Rests in Capitol." March 28, 1974.

———. "Young Girl's Diary." March 28, 1974.

Ellis, Gary. "Archaeologists Digging Up Fort King's Past." *Star Banner* (Ocala), January 1, 2003.

Fisher, W.L. "Old Town Brothers Are Descendants of Early Pioneer Settlers in State." *Advocate* (Dixie County), August 4, 1950.

Florida Sentinel (Tallahassee). "Obituary of Sarah Powell Chaires." March 17, 1846.

Floridian (Tallahassee). "Port of St. Marks." November 9, 1839.

———. "Sale of Fauntleroy." July 17, 1860.

Floridian and Advocate (Tallahassee). "An Abolitionist Caught." September 19, 1835.

———. "Assets of Central Bank." March 12, 1836.

———. "A Card." April 2, 1836.

———. "Chaires Announces Subscriptions for Leon Rail Road." June 12, 1832.

———. "Chaires a Reference for Attorney in Apalachicola." September 26, 1835.

———. "Chaires a Reference for Bridgeton High School." May 5, 1838.

———. "Chaires a 'Witness' against Duval." January 5, 1833.

———. "Chaires Declines Nomination to Constitutional Convention." September 25, 1838.

———. "Chaires Elected Director of Central Bank." January 10, 1835.

———. "Chaires Executor of Will of Davis Floyd." September 5, 1835.

———. "Chaires Has Mail at Tallahassee Post Office." October 16, 1832.

———. "Chaires on List of Candidates for Constitutional Convention." June 23, 1838.

———. "Chaires Presiding Justice in Leon County." April 20, 1833.

———. "Constitution of the Florida Agricultural Society." December 5, 1835.

———. "C.P. Chaires Representative to State Democratic Convention." April 14, 1860.

———. "C.P. Chaires Represents Natural Bridge at Democratic Meeting." April 9, 1860.

———. "Endorsement of Chaires for Constitutional Convention." March 17, 1838.

———. "Executor's Sale of Slaves and Goods of Davis Floyd." January 10, 1832.

———. "Florida Steam Packet Association Incorporated." March 10, 1838.

———. "From the Louisiana Journal." November 21, 1835.

———. "Hands Needed to Work on Tallahassee Rail Road." January 24, 1832.

———. "Hymeneal (Marriage of Mary Ann Chaires and William Burgess)." May 26, 1831.

———. "Joseph Chaires President of Florida-Georgia Plank Road Co." October 8, 1850.

———. "Listing of Central Bank Commissioners." February 23, 1832.

———. "Marshall's Sale of Railroad Lands and Equipment." August 21, 1841.

———. "Meeting at Shell Point." September 26, 1835.

———. "Notice of Mail at Tallahassee Post Office." October 3 and 17, 1835.

———. "Notice to File Claims on Chaires's Estate." October 13, 1838.

———. "Notice to Slaveholders." December 23, 1837.

———. "One of Three Planters Ready to Ship Cotton." September 27 and October 11, 1834.

———. "President of Fellenburg Institution." August 10, 1831.

———. "St. Andrews and Apalachicola Canal Company Incorporated." March 6, 1832.

———. "St. Joseph and Apalachicola." July 1, 1837.

———. "Take Him!" August 29, 1835.

Floridian and Journal (Tallahassee). "First Fair of the Leon County Agricultural Society." December 4, 1852.

———. "Obituary of Benjamin C. Burgess." July 21, 1860.

———. "Obituary of Benjamin Chaires." October 6, 1838.

———. "Chaires's Hamilton County Land for Sale." February 24, 1849.

———. "Notice." March 22, 1851.

Gazette (Apalachicola), "Obituary of Benjamin Chaires." October 20, 1838.

Gazette (Pensacola). "An Act Making Appropriations for the Indian Department." April 27, 1827.

———. "Bank of Florida in Tallahassee Incorporated." December 19, 1829.

———. "Duval and Chaires Recommend Extending Boundaries of Indian Land." May 27, 1826.

———. "Florida Land Agency Established." November 23, 1826.

Gordon, Crane & Co. "Proposals for Publishing at the Seat of Government, to be Entitled the Florida *Intelligencer*." *Gazette* (Pensacola), January 29, 1825.

Herald and Southern Democrat (St. Augustine). "Fruits of Peace (Chaires Massacre)." July 25, 1839.

———. "Letters at St. Augustine Post Office." January 11, 1823.

———. "Married (Joseph Chaires to Russell Ormond)." July 18, 1839.

Herald (St. Augustine). "Died (Obituary of Benjamin Chaires)." October 25, 1838.

Humphreys, G. "Proposals." *Gazette* (Pensacola), April 8, 1824.

Kennerly, Arthur. "Once Proud Chaires Mansion Now Lies in Ruins." *Democrat* (Tallahassee), March 4, 1956.

Land of Flowers (Tallahassee). "Obituary of C. P. Chaires." October 1881.

Manatee River Journal. "Story of Indian Attack at Braden Mansion." January 11, 1917.

Parkhill, John. "Notice of Subscription to Union Bank." *Floridian and Advocate* (Tallahassee), 1837, Volume 9, Issue 19.

Powell, Jeremiah. "Investigation of Magnolia Bank by the Legislative Council of Florida." *Floridian* (Tallahassee), January 27, 1834, Supplement.

Sentinel (Tallahassee). "Receipt for Advertising Sale of Chaires Lands by John A. Henderson." May 15, 1874.

Simmons, W.H., and John C. Cleland. "Notice to Land Claimants." *Florida Herald and Southern Democrat* (St. Augustine), August 8, 1839.

Star (Port St. Joe). "Historical Society Given Biography of Chaires Family." July 16, 1959.

Thompson, L.A. "State of the Condition of the Central Bank of Florida Sent to Governor Eaton (for 1835)." *Floridian and Advocate* (Tallahassee), 1836, Volume 7, Issue 31.

Times (St. Joseph). "Office of Lake Wimico and St. Joseph Canal and Railroad Co." September 26, 1838.

Weekly Floridian (Tallahassee). "Chaires and Wife Removed to Lake Como." September 16, 1879.

———. "A Good Opportunity." January 8, 1878.

———. "Lake Como Place Recently Destroyed by Fire." December 26, 1882.

———. "Obituary of Jackson J. Mash." August 20, 1885.

———. "An Old Landmark Gone." December 19, 1882.

———. "A Shooting Affray." November 18, 1879.

Yates, Steve. "Aging Columns Mark Site of Former Chaires Mansion." *Democrat* (Tallahassee), October 19, 1947.

Georgia Newspaper Articles

Chronicle (Augusta). "Appropriations Bill for Payment of Indian Rations." April 4, 1827.

———. "Gin House Blown Away." September 27, 1843.

Gazette and Republican Trumpet (Louisville). "Louisville Academy." August 21, 1804.

Georgian (Savannah). "Letters for B. Chaires." July 31 and August 7, 15, and 29, 1826.

———. "Mail for Benj. Chaires at Post Office." July 7, 1831.

Journal (Milledgeville). "Sale of Estate of Joseph Chaires." January 10, 1816.

Republican (Milledgeville). "Sale of Estate of Joseph Chaires." March 20, 1816.

Republican (Savannah). "Balances Due Tax Collector." February 25, 1809.

Times (Thomasville). "Furman Chaires's Wife Dies." April 18, 1885.

———. "Home Sold to Martha Chaires." October 10, 1903.

Weekly Telegraph (Macon). "Sale of Fauntleroy." August 27 and October 25, 1860.

———. "Westcott and Baltzell Duel." May 2, 1876.

Miscellaneous Newspaper Articles

City Gazette (Charleston). "Land Sales in Leon County." Running Advertisement. 1826.

Daily Herald (New Haven). "Description of Chaires Massacre." July 26, 1839, Volume 7, Issue 174.

Maps

Ball, LeRoy D., and Jne. Bradford. *Map of Leon County Showing Verdura owned by C. P. Chaires*. N.p.: n.p., 1883.

Chaires, Hank. "Memory Map." 1999.

Coffee, Joshua. *Location of Indian Agency Near Silver Springs*. In Kevin D. Kokomoor. "Indian agent Gad Humphreys and the Politics of slave claims on the Florida frontier, 1822-1830." Master's thesis, University of South Florida, 2008.

———. *Map of the Alachua Lands Claimed by Arredondo and Chaires*. Document from *Chaires v. United States*. 44 U.S. 3 How. 611 (1845).

Heiland, Sharyn. "Verdura Site Map." In "The Verdura Place: A Historical Overview and Preliminary Archaeological Survey." Master's thesis, Florida State University, 2001.

Leon County Survey, Township 1 South, Range 1 East, c1837. State Archives of Florida.

Map of Arredondo Grant. New York: Florida Land and Immigration Company, 1876.

Map of Leon County Showing Location of Verdura as a Tourist Attraction. Thomasville, GA: J. Rice Scott and W. H. Thames, 1930.

Map of North Addition to the City of Tallahassee, c1827. State Archives of Florida.

Map of Tallahassee and Leon County Showing Township and Range. Valdosta, GA: All States Map Company, c1980.

Plat of Martha Mash's Dower Settlement in T1S, R2E, 1895/6. Leon County Chancery Court Case 307. State Archives of Florida.

Royce, Charles O., Compiler. *Seminole Indian Reservation as Approved in 1823, Amended in 1824, and Re-Amended in 1827.* N.p.: n.p., 1896.

State of Florida, 1837. Port St. Joe, FL, Constitutional Convention Museum.

State of Florida. Washington, DC: Library of Congress, 1823.

State of Florida. Washington, DC: Library of Congress, 1829.

State of Florida. Washington, DC: Library of Congress, 1839.

State of Florida. Washington, DC: Library of Congress, 1846.

Survey Map of Township 1 South, Range 2 East (Based on 1801 Notes), 1824. State Archives of Florida.

Vickrey, Duke, Compiler. *Map of Wakulla County Showing Township and Range.* N.p.: n.p., 2000.

View of the City of Tallahassee, State Capital of Florida, 1885. State Archives of Florida.

Woodville and Lafayette Quadrangle. Washington, DC: U.S. Department of the Interior, 1981.

U.S. Government Documents on GenealogyBank.com

The following sources were found using genealogybank.com. "SSV" refers to "Serial Set Volume," a finding tool on that site.

Comptroller of the Treasury. "Balances on Books of the Third Auditor." 1838. SSV 346.

Congress. "Approval of an Act for the Appropriation of Land for Two Academies." May 4, 1836. SSV 283.

House of Representatives. "An Act to Incorporate the Chipola Canal Company." February 29, 1828. SSV 172.

———. "A Bill Supplementary to the Act Authorizing the Territory of Florida to Open Canals between Chipola River and St. Andrews Bay." March 2, 1831. SSV 214.

———. "A Bill Supplementary to the Act Authorizing the Territory of Florida to Open Canals between Chipola River and St. Andrews Bay." April 27, 1832. SSV 214.

Secretary of the Interior. "Response to Letter from Joseph Chaires Sent to Valentine Conway." 1843. SSV 2167.

Secretary of the Treasurer. "Report on Private Land Claims in East Florida Communicated to the Senate." January 18, 1830. SSV 192.

———. "Statement of the Condition of the Central Bank of Florida (for 1837)." 1838. SSV 319.

———. "Testimony of Antonio Alverez, Taken under Commission in the Cases of Benjamin Chaires and Others... against the United States." 1836. SSV 286.

Secretary of War. "Disbursements of Moneys, &c. for the Benefit of the Indians." 1834. SSV 259.

———. "Disbursements to the Indians, Copies of Accounts." 1827. SSV 156.

———. "Disbursements to the Indians, Copies of Accounts." 1830. SSV 197.

———. "Information about Florida Indians Including Contract with Chaires." 1826. SSV 149.

———. "Letter from Governor Duval to the Secretary of War." 1825. SSV 134.

———. "Letter to Col. Thos. McKenney, General Superintendent of Indian Affairs." 1826. SSV 134.

———. "Regarding Bribe of Pindar by Chaires." 1826. SSV 149.

———. "Regarding Contract Proposals and Chaires Contract." 1826. SSV 134.

———. "Statement of Contracts Made during the Year 1833." 1834. SSV 256.

————. "Trade and Intercourse with the Indians." 1826. SSV 137.

————. "Treaty with the Florida Indians." 1826. SSV 134.

Treasurer. "Statement of the Balances in the Hands of Agents for Paying Pensions." December 5, 1837. SSV 314.

————. "Treasurer's Accounts for 2nd and 3rd Quarters of 1836." 1837. SSV 321.

U.S. Government Documents on Ancestry.com

Federal Census. Levy County, Florida. 1870.

————. Pulaski County, Georgia. 1820.

————. Queen Anne's County, Maryland. 1790.

————. Murderkill 100, Delaware. 1800, 1810.

General Land Office. Certificate of the Commissioner of the Land Office in Tallahassee, Florida, 1826. U.S. General Land Office Records, 1796-1907.

Miscellaneous

Ancestry.com. http://www.ancestry.com.

"The Birth of a Settlement." *City of Holly Hill*. http://www.hollyhillfl.org/about/history.

Brandon, Harriet Jones. Letter to James A. Brandon, March 6, 1879. Thomas County Historical Society.

CensusRecords.com. http://www.censusrecords.com.

Chaires, E. Ellington and George Lester Patterson. The Genealogy of the Chaires Family, n.d. Personal collection of Daniel Fletcher.

Chaires, Hank. Interview by Sharyn Heiland. September 10, 1999.

Collection of Various Family Papers. Personal collection of Daniel Fletcher.

"Courts and the Establishment of New Counties: First Act of the Territorial Legislature, 1822." *Floripedia.* http://fcit.usf.edu/Florida/docs/c/courts.htm.

"Deed Record A." *Alachua County.* http://www.alachuaclerk.org/archive.

"Deed Record I-J." *Alachua County.* http://www.alachuaclerk.org/archive.

"Descendants Search." *Daughters of the American Revolution.* http://services.dar.org/public/dar_research.

Family Bible Record of Thomas Butler Chaires and Sallie Salter Chaires, Copied by Virginia Chaires Webb, June 11, 1964. Personal collection of Daniel Fletcher.

FindaGrave.com. http://www.findagrave.com.

"Florida Confederate Soldiers Bundle." *Civil War Microfilm.* http://www.civilwarmicrofilm.com/products.php#1.

Florida Department of Environmental Protection. *Constitutional Convention, 1835-1837.* State museum pamphlet and displays. N.p.: Florida Department of Environmental Protection, n.d.

Johnson, James B., compiler. "The Chaires Family." www.angelfire.com/flacracker (website no longer available).

Landry, Elsa, and Hazel Landry. Genealogy of the Chaires Family (Florida Branch). Personal collection of George Lester.

Old Salt Works. *A Little History (of Port St. Joe)*. Tourist information. N.p.: n.p., n.d.

Pugsley, Edwin. Dear Mr. Conrad: Letter Written from Edgewood Plantation in Monticello, FL. Personal collection of Daniel Fletcher.

Records of the Disposition of Destitute Orphans, 1878. City Archives, New Orleans Public Library. Transcription at http://nutrias.org/inv/orphans%201878.htm.

"Symptoms of Yellow Fever." *Health Grades*. http://www.rightdiagnosis.com/y/yellow_fever/symptoms.htm.

St. Johns County. Florida County Circuit Court Collections. Case 155-20. St. Augustine Historical Society.

"Treaty of Amity, Settlement, and Limits between the United States of America and His Catholic Majesty, 1819." *Yale Law School*. http://avalon.law.yale.edu/19th_century/sp1819.asp.

University of Georgia. *Centennial Alumni Catalogue*. Athens: University of Georgia, 1901.

Wakulla County. Deed Record Numbers A195, B390, E382, and GHI372. Crawfordville, FL Clerk of Court.

War Department, Adjutant General. Letter to House of Representatives, The Honorable Tom Yon. 1930.

WorldVitalRecords.com. http://www.worldvitalrecords.com.

Wright, L.M. Joseph Chaires in Georgia: Note among Papers
  Concerning the Life of Benjamin Chaires. Personal
  collection of Daniel Fletcher.

INDEX

Adams, Drucilla, 163
Alachua Lands, 23, 39-55, 93, 138, 146
Allen, R. C., 33, 37, 65
Alligator Creek, 43- 45, 49, 53-54
Amelia Island, 9-10, 13, 24-25, 50, 55-56, 145
American Revolution, 2, 4, 28, 73
Apalachee Indians, 31
Arredondo Grant, 40, 50
Arredondo, Fernando de la Maza, 25
Arredondo, Jose de la Maza, 39-51, 53-54
Ashton, John, 28-29

Bannerman Place, 109
Beach Plantation, 9, 13, 24, 145
Bel-Air, 92
Bellamy, John, 19, 33
Berry, Robert, 81, 145-146
Betton, Turbett R., 58, 64, 69, 71
Big Hammock, 18, 42-55
Big Swamp. *See* Big Hammock
Bolton Plantation, 91, 189
Britt, O.W., 137
Burgess, Benjamin Chaires 62, 79, 89-90, 106, 108, 147, 153, 156-159, 162, 189
Burgess, Mary Ann Chaires. *See* Chaires, Mary Ann
Burgess Tract, 60, 128, 157, 187
Burgess, William Gaither, 37, 62, 64, 89-90, 153-157, 162
Burgess, William Gaither, Jr., 89-90, 106, 108, 153-154, 156
Burgevin, Andres, 42-55
Butler, Robert, 10-11, 34, 73
Butler, Thomas, 25, 50, 106

C.P. and T.B. Chaires, 126
C.P. Chaires & Co., 126
Cabbage Swamp, 14, 25-26, 55
Call, Richard Keith, 33-34, 63, 65, 69, 73, 87
Call's Railroad, 63
Campbell, Duncan G., 10-11
Cascades, 31
Cedar Keys, 124-127, 130, 187-188
Central Bank of Florida, 33, 58-59, 69-72, 88, 138
Chaires
    ancestry chart, 141
    family scandal, 123, 127-132
    French ancestry, 2, 141
    loss of Verdura by, 90, 134
    pronunciation of, 2
Chaires, Alice Burroughs, 99, 170, 172
Chaires & Co., 126
Chaires, Benjamin
    as banker, 58-59, 69-73, 137
    as brick maker, 56-57, 59
    as major land holder, 38-39
    as millionaire, 138
    as slave owner, 77-87
    as trustee on University of Florida Board of Trustees, 74
    character of, 87-89
    confusion with Benjamin Chaires, Sr., 92
    education of, 4, 33
    in court, 26-29
    land owned at time of death, 90-91
    military involvement of, 74-75
    nomination of to Constitutional Convention, 73
    obituary of, xiii, 87
    portrait of, 1
Chaires, Benjamin Cadwallader, 60, 75, 92, 128-134, 151, 167-175, 186, 197
Chaires, Benjamin, Jr., 6, 75, 89, 128, 130, 143, 167-170, 186

232

Chaires, Bradford, 99-100, 103-105, 132

Chaires, Charles, 2

Chaires, Charles Moore, 1-3, 5-6

Chaires, Charles Powell, 123-135, 193
    as owner of Verdura, 90, 95
    birth of, 32, 89, 123
    burial of, 90, 106, 132
    business firms of, 126
    death of, 89, 132
    dispersal of estate, 132-134
    hand in establishing a public library, 133
    incarceration of, 127
    marriage of, 123, 126
    shooting encounter with Benjamin Cadwallader, 131
    slaves owned by, 112-113
    value of personal property of, 124

Chaires, Charles Robert, 60, 145-146, 151-152, 171

Chaires, Furman 13, 89-91, 106, 123, 130, 143, 146, 161, 169, 177-178

Chaires, Green D.
    birth of, 6, 89, 161
    burial of, 90, 106, 163
    children of, 106, 108, 132, 161
    death of, 55, 89, 163
    grandchildren of, 104, 106
    marriage of, 106, 161, 163
    obituary of, 163
    timeline of, 161-163

Chaires, Green Hill, 1-3, 5-7, 32, 38, 59-60, 62, 77-80, 92, 121, 145, 153-154

Chaires, Henry Agnew "Hank," 99, 104, 110-111

Chaires, John. *See* Chare, Jan de la

Chaires, Joseph (Benjamin's father), 1-3, 5

Chaires, Joseph (Benjamin's son)
    as administrator of father's estate, 50, 68, 90, 92-93
    as banker, 137

birth of, 6, 89, 145
burial of, 90, 147-148
death of, 89, 146
epitaph of, 148
obituary of, 147-148
timeline of, 145-147
Chaires, Joseph Scott, 1-3, 5, 7, 138
Chaires, Josephine, 32, 89-90, 106, 108, 143, 195
Chaires, Martha, 32, 89, 91, 143, 146, 156, 161, 177, 189-191
Chaires, Mary Ann, 6, 37, 62, 79-80, 89-90, 106, 108, 143, 145,
    153-156
Chaires, Mary Green. *See* Green, Mary
Chaires Mills, 3, 7
Chaires, Octavia, 130
Chaires, Polly Green, 145-146, 150
Chaires, Samuel Parkhill, 99, 130, 132-133, 161-162, 164-165,
    171-172
Chaires, Sarah Jane, 14, 33, 89, 91, 102, 137, 143, 181-183
Chaires, Sarah Powell. *See* Powell, Sarah
Chaires, Thomas Butler
    as owner of Verdura, 91, 95, 98, 123
    birth of, 32, 89, 185
    burial of, 90, 106
    business firms of, 126
    death of, 89, 187
    namesake of, 25
    slaves owned by, 110, 112-113, 119
    timeline of, 185-188
Chaires, Thomas Peter, 1, 3, 38, 92, 121
Chare, Jan de la, 2, 141
Civil War, 23, 75, 91, 113, 119, 121-122, 125, 169
Clarke, George J. F., 45, 54
Coffee, Joshua A., 46-48, 51-54
Columns, 57-59, 70, 111, 138
Coppinger, Jose, 25, 41-42, 53
Cornucopia, 92

Cotton Kingdom, 89, 95, 118, 122
Creek Indians, 4, 31
Croom, Bryan, 109
Cross Creek, 39
Crupper, Micajah, 18, 20-22

Diego Plains, 8, 10, 13-14, 25-26, 50, 55
Dresser, Amos, 83-86
Duval County Courthouse, 14
Duval, Robert, 87
Duval, William, 13, 17-22, 34, 69, 73

East Florida lands, 138
El Destino Plantation, 109
Ever May, 91, 105, 110, 123, 127-130, 133-134, 171-172, 187,
    193
Evergreen Hill, 92

Fatio, Francis, 25-26, 40, 46, 48
Fauntleroy Plantation, 37, 91-92, 109, 130, 133, 146, 167-172
Fauntleroy, George, 69, 80-81, 91
Fellenburg Institute, 73, 85
Fenn, Mary, 7
Fitch, Thomas, 9-10, 25-27, 77, 85, 185
Fletcher, Daniel, 101, 103
Florida Agricultural Society, 56
Florida Constitutional Convention, xv, 68, 73, 88
Florida *Intelligencer*, 35
Florida Land Agency, 33-34, 73-74
Florida State University, 57, 74, 101
Florida Steam Packet Association Company, 69
Florida Territorial Legislative Council, 13, 15, 31, 34, 36, 60,
    63-64, 69-70, 72-74
Forbes Purchase, 91
Fort King, 46, 53
Fraser, John, 26-27

Gadsden, James, 33-34, 73-74
Gamble, Robert Howard, 65, 91, 157, 189-191
Georgia Land Lotteries, 5
Godwin, Catherine, 1
Goodwood, 109
Green, Mary, 1-2
Greenfield Plantation, 26

Halifax lands, 25, 50, 55, 145, 185
Henderson, John A., 23, 55, 92-93, 164
Henry the Carriage Driver. *See* Richardson, Henry
Humphreys, Gad, 18-21, 32, 40

Indian massacre at Evergreen Hill, 2, 92
Indian rations, 18-22
Indian reservations, 16-18, 48, 87-88

Jackson, Andrew, 15, 21, 33, 35, 87
Jacksonville, planning of, 13-14, 87
James Madison Institute, 57
Jones, William Thomas, 10, 29

Kingsley, Zephaniah, 26-28

Lake Wimico and St. Joseph Canal and Railroad Company, 64-66, 68, 137
Leon Railroad Company, 63
Leon Rail-Way Company, 63
Louisville Academy, 4
Louisville town plans, 7, 87

Magnolia, 59-61
Mash, Henry Terrell, 128-129, 171
Mash, Jackson J., 126
Mash, Mamie. *See* Mash, Martha
Mash, Martha, 126-135, 162, 164, 170-171

Mash, Mattie. *See* Mash, Martha
May Place. *See* Ever May
McGirtt's Point, 28-29
McIntosh, John, 28-29
McKenney, Thomas, 21
Merchants and Planters Bank of Magnolia, 69-72
Milledgeville town plans, 7, 87
Mintz, Anne, 102
Miranda, Pedro, 40, 46-48, 54
Monroe, James, 17-18, 187
Mt. Vernon, 56-57, 138
Munro, Robert J., 137

Nucleus, 32-36, 38, 72-73, 88-89

Ormand, Russell, 106, 108, 145-146, 149-150

Panic of 1837, 37
Parkhill, Ann Maria, 106, 161, 165
Parkhill, John, 65, 92
Patriot War, 41, 74
Pichard, Gordon, 137
Pindar, Charles, 21
Plank Road Company, 60, 146, 161
plantations, status factors of, 118-121
Powell, Sarah, 3, 6, 80, 83, 89-90, 106-108, 143-144, 155, 195

Raines, Sarah Ann (Sallie), 106, 123-125
Revolutionary War. *See* American Revolution
Richardson, Henry, 80, 85, 107

Saints, 35, 64, 89
Salter, Sarah (Sallie), 106, 185, 187-188
Seminole Indians, 16, 37, 41, 46, 88, 91
Seminole Wars, 15
sharecropping, 113-122

slavery
  add for sale of slaves, 81-82
  and the construction of St. Augustine Road, 78
  at Verdura (*see* Verdura Plantation, slaves at)
  Chaires's slaves' names, 77-81
  quality of slaves' lives, 83-86
  runaway slaves, 15-16
slave holdings in Florida, 119-120
slave owner resolution, 84-85
Southern Rights Association of Roache's Crossroad and Natural
  Bridge, 124
Southwood Plantation, 91, 102, 181-183
Spanish Land Grants, 22-24, 45, 50
St. Andrews and Chipola Canal and Rail Road Company, 64
St. Joe Paper Company, 95, 101, 110, 117, 134, 137
St. Joseph and Iola Railroad, 67-68, 73, 79, 137

T.B. and C.P. Chaires, 130
T.B. Chaires & Co., 126
Tallahassee Railroad, 60, 63, 69, 79, 125. *See also* Call's
  Railroad
Union Bank, 33, 72, 145, 181
Tappan, Arthur, 84
taxes and ordinances, suspension of, 13
tenant farmers, 113-122
tenant structures, 116-117
Territorial Legislative Council, 13, 15
Theus-Roberts Farm, 109
Thompson, Leslie A., 33, 35, 71, 79, 88
Tiger Tail, 91, 110, 123, 185, 187
Treaty of Moultrie Creek, 16, 18, 48

Union Bank, 33, 70, 72, 138, 145, 181
University of Florida, 74

Verdura Place. *See* Verdura Plantation
Verdura Plantation, 95-122
    advertisement for sale of, 98, 125
    archaeology at, 100-101
    as elite/upper-class plantation, 118-122
    boundaries of, 95
    buildings at, 95-96
    comparison to Pine Hill, 98-99
    description of house at, 96-100
    drawing of mansion at, 103
    end of ownership of by the Chaires, 134
    fate of, 137
    fire at, 104-105
    future of, 138
    graveyard at, 90, 105-108
    location of, 91, 95
    naming of, 95
    ruins of, 96-97
    site map of, 102
    slaves at 78, 109-113
    social and economic decline at, 122

War of 1812, 11, 24, 74-75
Ward, George T., 33, 86, 91, 102, 181-183, 189
Webb, Virginia Chaires, 106
Westcott, James D., 33, 64, 88
Wiggins, Daniel, 2, 97
Williams, Robert W., 37, 69, 134, 137
Willis, Jesse, 56, 65, 80
Woodlawn, 92, 111
Wright, Nathaniel, 1

Yellow Fever, xiii, 10, 68, 87, 89, 106, 132, 146
Yonge, Phillip Robert, 26